# DISCIPLING:
## THE MULTIPLYING MINISTRY

AN ANALYSIS OF MULTIPLYING D̶I̶S̶CIPLESHIP
IN THE MINISTRY O̶F̶
AND ITS APPLICATIO̶N̶ ̶T̶O̶ ̶T̶H̶E̶ ̶C̶H̶URCH

Foreword by Joe R. Barnett

Published By
Star Bible & Tract Corp. • Ft. Worth, TX  76118

# ACKNOWLEDGEMENTS

*My special thanks to my parents, Jimmie and Helen Jones, who never stopped encouraging me, to my wife Barbie, who faithfully stood by me, to Jack Paul, who gave me a new vision, and to those brothers I've discipled (**you** are what this book is all about). Thanks also to Regina Buckley for her work in the initial preparation of this manuscript, and to Clifford Cone and Randy Prude who have given me so much support. Thanks, Bill, for allowing me to bounce these concepts off of you so many times.*

Cover design by Kent Pate

Illustrations by Marla Imus.

ISBN 0-933672-78-0

First Printing, 1982 — 25,000
Second Printing, 1985 — 25,000

One man awake,
Awakens another.
The second awakens
His next-door brother.
The three awake
Can rouse a town
By turning the whole place
Upside down.
The many awake
Can make such a fuss
It finally awakens the rest of us.
One man up
With dawn in his eyes
Multiplies.

— Helen Kromer

# — CONTENTS —

Page

Foreword ..................................... 5

Chapter 1
The Problem With Discipleship ............. 7

Chapter 2
Defining A Disciple ........................ 15

Chapter 3
The Task of the Disciple .................. 29

Chapter 4
The Multiplying Ministry ................... 41

Chapter 5
Multiplication in the New Testament ....... 49

Chapter 6
The Four-Phase Following ................. 69

Chapter 7
Levels of Relationship ...................... 79

Chapter 8
Applying The Levels ........................ 87

Chapter 9
Relational and Terminal Thinking .......... 99

Chapter 10
The Cost of Discipleship .................. 113

Chapter 11
Barriers To Discipleship .................. 125

Chapter 12
Selection Is The Key ...................... 133

Chapter 13
Some Concluding Thoughts .............. 149

Bibliography ................................. 153

# — FOREWORD —

## By Joe R. Barnett

This has to be one of the most revolutionary books ever written by one of our people.

According to recent studies, if churches of Christ continue at the same growth rate experienced during the past decade, we will reach the end of this century one-half our present numerical size. If, however, the principles of this book are applied, we will come to the year 2000 many times our present numerical and spiritual strength.

This book is more travelogue than research.

It is more experience than theory.

More heart than head.

More commitment than technique.

That's not a put down. It's the highest recommendation I could give.

Milton Jones is a bright, thoughtful person. An outstanding student. So all the secondary items mentioned above can be found in this work. It is the product of careful research. It contains theory, thought, and technique.

But it is much more.

I first met the author when he was a student at Texas Tech University and I was minister for the Broadway Church of Christ. He was actively involved in the student ministry, and won more of his fellow students to Christ than anyone I had ever observed.

Frankly, I didn't understand how he did it. He was friendly, but shy. He seemed to listen more than he talked. He didn't move in a whirlwind of organized-to-the-minute activity. But he got the job done.

The students he reached were soon reaching others. And that's the thesis of this book. *Discipleship.*

According to the author discipleship involves three things: evangelizing, edifying, and equipping. If we could come to terms with this point it would turn us around.

The book could be entitled "Beyond Baptism" because the author focuses on the two parts of the Great Commission: 1) winning people to Christ, and 2) making disciples of them.

He explains the principle of multiplication — shows how it worked in New Testament days and how it will work today. He gives us hope by focusing on multiplying the workers rather than looking at the seemingly hopeless ratio of church members to world population.

The author does an outstanding job of "applying" scripture. He looks at what Jesus did, and applies it, pleading for a duplication of Jesus' method.

It will cause the reader to ask some hard questions, mostly self-directed. I doubt you can read it without self-evaluation. And I suspect it will make you a bit uncomfortable. But I also believe you will come away from this reading with the feeling that this is no gimmick. It doesn't offer a "pie-in-the-sky" program — just an in-depth study of scripture and its application.

I recommend the book without reservation for two reasons:

First, I have read it and believe it is accurate. The appeal is to scripture; to a rebirth of the principles which caused Christianity to spread so rapidly and so far in the first century.

Secondly, I know the author. He is no fanatic. He doesn't regard himself the savior of the church. He has no ax to grind. He loves the brotherhood. He practices what he preaches. That's why I said the book is more travelogue than research. Milton Jones has tested what he writes about here. In a sense this is his travelogue, his spiritual journey.

Our Lord gave us a job to do. We haven't done it. Perhaps because we haven't known how. When you finish this book you'll know how. And I think we will do the job.

# THE PROBLEM WITH DISCIPLESHIP

1

E ver since Jesus made those striking words to "Go therefore and make disciples of all the nations baptizing them in the name of the Father and the Son and the Holy Spirit" (Matt. 28:19)[1], Christians have been perplexed with the problem of how to fulfill this commandment. Many have counted the charge an impossibility, and others obviously have not been doing it. This has been true of churches in the past and also of those today. Possibly the greatest reason this problem has existed is because there has generally been a lack of understanding concerning that phrase "make disciples."

Churches have been searching for a method or a gimmick that would help them to win the world to Christ but have virtually ignored the plan that was mapped out by Jesus Himself. The Great Commission cannot be done if it is not done in the manner of the Master, and His plan is to make disciples. Many churches have launched great schemes with good intentions and sincere hearts, and yet the job still has not been done. Robert Coleman states: "Merely because we are busy, or even skilled, doing something does not necessarily mean that we are getting anything accomplished. The question must always be asked: Is it worth doing? And does it get the job done?"[2]

Probably the biggest problem has been that there has neither been a proper understanding of who composes "a disciple" nor what it means to "make disciples." It is difficult to accomplish a task if one does not understand the objective or the means to the goal. When it is studied, it becomes evident that the reason churches have not been fulfilling the Great Commission is because they have not been doing it Jesus' way.

As Matthew 28:19-20 is read, one must notice that Christ's commission to His church was not to "make converts" or to put another notch on one's evangelistic belt, but it was to "make disciples." It is possible to have evangelistic methods that reach thousands of people and still not have any maturing Christians. The gospel can be proclaimed, and there still be the failure to make disciples.

Jesus spent about three and one-half years in His public ministry. During this time, He preached the message of the Kingdom of God, He taught the people who He was, and He performed miracles to authenticate His claims. Jesus also spent a great amount of His time in the training of twelve men. They spent time with Him in all types of life situations and learned from His example how to relate to God and work with people. After the public ministry of Jesus, two things had been accomplished. First, He had filled the minds of the multitudes with His teachings. Secondly, He had prepared a small group of men who were trained and would be ready after the ascension to gather in the harvest. These followers were given the commission to "make disciples." Wherever these believers went they followed in the pattern of Jesus and the twelve, and they made disciples.

Jesus concentrated most of His time on making a few disciples, and these men were taught to do the same. Through the process of multiplication, the gospel was to spread throughout the world. It is unfortunate that so few understand this process today. Even church leaders have lost sight of that charge to teach others to observe all things that Jesus commanded.

8

# BACKGROUND OF THE STUDY

By studying the word, "disciple," one can find that it is used in various ways. Most equate "disciples" with "Christians." However, there is no more reason to equate these two words than there is to equate the titles, "Lord" and "Christ." These two titles can both refer to the same person, Jesus, but their meanings are different. Similarly, "disciple" and "Christian" can and should refer to the same person, but their meanings can also be different. This can be seen in the early church when "the disciples were first called Christians in Antioch" (Acts 11:26). Today, most believers in Christ refer to themselves as Christians. Although they wear the name "Christian" which implies that they have been saved and are of the Christ, the anointed one, often their lives hardly measure up to the identifying characteristics of a "disciple" as described in the New Testament. In the early church the disciples were called Christians, but the question for this study is — "Can 'Christians' today be called disciples?"

The process of "evangelizing" has also been equated with "discipling" or "making disciples." This also poses a problem because someone can be doing both of these, but they are not necessarily the same thing. Evangelism is a part of making disciples, but it is not the totality of the commission.

Those few disciples upon whom Jesus had concentrated His attention had learned what it meant to make disciples. Jesus had made disciples of them. They had learned of Him and had followed in His steps. When Jesus asked them to "go and make disciples," they knew what He meant because He was merely asking them to continue what He had practiced with them. Jesus knew that this plan would not fail because the disciples were conformed to their Master, and they would reproduce His life in others.

Jesus' first disciples understood the concept of

9

discipleship because they had been discipled by Him. It is difficult to understand the concept of discipleship, if one has never been discipled. The reason that the meanings of "disciple" and "making disciples" are foreign to many believers is because many Christians over the years have been evangelizing without making disciples. Jesus' commission includes both, and it is imperative to look at Jesus' plan rather than the many processes of churches in the past which have not produced multiplying disciples as an end result.

## IMPORTANCE OF THE STUDY

The importance of understanding discipleship is well stated by Gene Getz:

> Anyone who attempts to formulate a biblical philosophy of the ministry and develop a contemporary strategy, a methodology that stands foursquare on scriptural foundations must ask and answer a very fundamental question. Why does the church exist? Why has God let it in the world in the first place?

> The Bible has not left us without the answer. Jesus Christ, before ascending to the Father, spoke directly to this question. One day on a mountain in Galilee He spoke in clear and simple language. "Go therefore and make disciples of all the nations, baptizing them in the name of the Father and the Son and the Holy Spirit, teaching them to observe all that I commanded you; and lo, I am with you always, even to the end of the age" (Matt. 28:19-20)[3]

The Apostle Peter said "there is salvation in no one else; for there is no other name under heaven that has been given among men, by which we must be saved" (Acts 4:12). Since one can only be saved through faith in Jesus, most of the world is lost. The only way the world can be won to Christ is by doing it Jesus' way — making disciples. The world appears to be such a gigantic mission that it would be impossible to truly make an impact on it. Only the discipleship method is able to do so because it multiplies people.

There are various other reasons for holding to the importance of the Great Commission. First, it is a command for all Christians; it is not optional. It is also important because it helps believers reach maturity in Christ. Many only acquire a nominal belief in Jesus and never move to maturity in their relationship with Him. Others start following Jesus, and then fall away. Considering the promise that Jesus will return, there is also a sense of urgency to this command. Gene Warr was committed to the commission for these three reasons: (1) the brevity of life, (2) a sense of stewardship, and, (3) his desire to have his life count for something worthwhile.[4]

## PURPOSE OF THE STUDY

The purpose of this study is fourfold: (1) to understand what discipleship meant in a New Testament context, (2) to explore the plan of Jesus' method of discipleship exhibited in the training of the twelve and carried forward in the Acts of the Apostles, (3) to evaluate the present situation concerning the process of making disciples in churches today in light of the New Testament example, and (4) to apply Jesus' method of discipling to churches and individual Christians today. This study intends to seek a missing ingredient in most churches and to offer recommendations to believers in order to see a change in the world situation as a result of a tremendous impact through multiplying discipleship.

## QUESTIONS TO BE ANSWERED

This study will attempt to answer the following questions:

1. What are discipleship and discipling?
2. What is Jesus' method for winning the world to Him?
3. How does a disciple relate to God, to other people, and his activities to his purpose?

4. How does a multiplying discipleship ministry fit into the life of a Christian and the function of the church today?

# DEFINITION OF TERMS

The following terms will be defined extensively in this study, but in order to begin, some short workable definitions are needed.

## Disciple

A learner who has conformed his mind, words, and actions to that of his Master.

## Discipling

Discipling others is the process by which a Christian with a life worth emulating commits himself for an extended period of time to a few individuals who have been won to Christ, the purpose being to aid and guide their growth to maturity and equip them to reproduce in *at least* a third spiritual generation.[5]

## Multiplying Discipleship

The process by which disciples reproduce according to geometric ratio.

# QUESTIONS

1. If we are to fulfill the Great Commission, how must it be done?
2. After the public ministry of Jesus, what two things had been done?
3. Do you think that everyone who calls himself a "Christian" is truly a disciple? Explain.
4. Why has this concept of "making disciples" become foreign to many Christians today?
5. What are some reasons for committing to the Great Commission of making disciples?
6. How do you fit into the Great Commission?

# FOOTNOTES

[1] All Bible references are from the New American Standard Bible translation unless otherwise indicated.

[2] Robert Coleman, *The Master Plan of Evangelism* (Old Tappan: Fleming H. Revell, 1963), p. 11.

[3] Gene Getz, *Sharpening the Focus of the Church* (Chicago: Moody Press, 1974), p. 21.

[4] Gene Warr, *You Can Make Disciples* (Waco: Word Books, 1978), pp. 69-70.

[5] Allen Hadidian, *Successful Discipling* (Chicago: Moody Press, 1979), pp. 29-30. Words in italics are my own qualification.

# DEFINING A DISCIPLE

2

## MORE THAN A PUPIL

The history of the usage of $\mu\alpha\theta\eta\tau\grave{\eta}s$ is diverse and interesting. It has been translated as disciple, apprentice, student, learner, and pupil. The King James Version is consistent and always translates this word as disciple, but some of the other versions have opted for alternate renderings. A good example is found in Luke 6:40 in the New American Standard Bible: "A pupil is not above his teacher; but everyone, after he has been fully trained, will be like his teacher." The New International Version translates the word, "student." When the background of $\mu\alpha\theta\eta\tau\grave{\eta}s$ is reviewed, it becomes apparent that a $\mu\alpha\theta\eta\tau\grave{\eta}s$ is more than a pupil or a student. It is at least more than the concept that many have of pupils today. According to modern usage, a pupil or student is merely one who studies or one who is under the care of a guardian. However, in ancient usage, the $\mu\alpha\theta\eta\tau\grave{\eta}s$ (from this point on translated "disciple") was far more than this current definition.

A "disciple" is nearly always used in conjunction with the word, "teacher." A disciple is contrasted with a pupil because a disciple conforms his mind to that of his teacher.[1] Everyone who has gone to school for any time has sat under a teacher from whom he has learned, but that does not necessarily mean he has conformed his mind to that of his teacher. The student may not have conformed his mind because the teacher was wrong, because the teacher was boring, because the teacher was a hypocrite, or simply because the student had not the desire. Many students today learn from a teacher simply to be able to pass a course, and there is not an intimate teacher/student relationship at all.

In contrast to the previous situation, a disciple has a direct dependence upon his teacher.[2] The goal of a disciple/teacher relationship is more than just to pick up certain information or direction, but it is to have fellowship with him.[3] The Greek philosophers understood well the concept of discipleship. Plato could be described as a disciple of Socrates. Socrates' disciples were overwhelmed with him, and they listened to every word he spoke and watched every action that he did in order to be prepared to teach others.[4] The basis of the relationship was Socrates himself rather than the knowledge he had at his disposal. He was the master around whom his disciples gathered. Disciples who were young and old gathered around Socrates because he was granting to them fellowship and allowing them to share in his life.[5] Thus, a disciple became one who conformed all of his mind, words, and actions to that of his teacher. In this context, Jesus' words in Luke 6:40 take on a stronger significance: "A disciple is not above his teacher; but when he is fully trained he will be like his teacher" (Phillips).

The groups who had congregated and had been discipled by the Greek philosophers of antiquity did not just wither away after their teacher was gone. When their teacher left or died, he still lived because he was alive in his disciples. The disciples had conformed their lives to that of their teacher in order that he might live. The system worked. Plato, the disciple of Socrates, founded the Academy where their philosophy and science continued to be taught for 900 years.[6] This same phenomenon can be seen in Jesus after His ascension. Jesus had left the earth in bodily form, but He lived because He lived in His disciples who were conformed to Him.

In the New Testament, a true disciple is one who has attached himself to Jesus as his Master. This attachment shapes the entirety of the disciple's life. The relationship is not bound up in knowledge of facts as much as it is in the person of Jesus Christ. It is the responsibility and privilege of the disciple to be like Him. As they become like Him, they will live to reproduce Him in other people. This is the type of discipleship that must exist in churches today if indeed the Great Commission to "make disciples" is to be obeyed.

> Christian discipleship is a teacher-student relationship, based on the model of Christ and His disciples, in which the teacher reproduces the fullness of life he has in Christ in the student so well, that the student is able to train others to teach others.[7]

## FORMS TO THE REAL JESUS

The song sung by children puts it well:

> To be like Jesus, to be like Jesus
> All I want, to be like Him.

This is the goal of discipleship — to be like Jesus. Thomas a Kempis stated this important principle in his classic, *Of The Imitation of Christ:*

> "He that followeth me, shall not walk in darkness" (John 8:12), saith the Lord. These are the words of Christ, by which we are admonished how we ought to imitate His life and manners, if we would be enlightened and delivered from all blindness of heart. Let therefore our chief endeavor be to meditate upon the life of Jesus Christ . . . But whosoever will fully and with relish understand the words of Christ must endeavor to conform his life wholly to the life of Christ.[8]

If disciples are to be like Jesus, then it is imperative for disciples to know the real Jesus. It is impossible for "disciples" to be conformed to the image of His Son (Romans 8:29), if they do not have a good conception of who He is. Jesus' first disciples had the opportunity of walking, talking, and spending time with Him while He was in bodily form. Disciples in the present century do not have this same privilege. However, it is still necessary for them to know and imitate the same Jesus.

It is possible today to have a false conception of Jesus. A person could even think that he is following Jesus when he is not. One might be practicing a modern day idolatry by following and worshipping a misconception of Jesus. A disciple must follow and be like the real Jesus and not his own personal view of Jesus or one that he has inherited.

Disciples today must seek to know the Jesus of the gospels. He must seek Him out of Matthew, Mark, Luke and John in order to find the true and only teacher worthy of imitation and exaltation. The gospels do not tell everything about Jesus, but they tell enough. "Many other signs therefore Jesus also performed in the presence of the disciples, which are not written in this book; but these have been written that you may believe that Jesus is the Christ, the Son of God; and that believing you may have life in His name" (John 20:30-31). The gospels are not complete biographies, but if they are studied, a sufficient knowledge of Jesus can be obtained in order to present an example for emulation.

Disciples must conform to the true Jesus of the gospels. R.T. France speaks of portraits of Jesus that are not complete:

> Many other Jesuses have been invented. The liberal theologians of the last century invented a sentimental Jesus who was all for peace and harmony and social justice, the great preacher of the fatherhood of God and the brotherhood of men. The modern humanist invents a

Jesus who is the supreme example of self-giving service to his fellow-men. Many of us have been brought up on an anaemic Jesus, friend of little children, incapable of any angry thought or divisive action.

All these Jesuses contain some genuine features, of course. Jesus did preach the virtues of love and forgiveness; he did attack exploitation and injustice; he is the supreme example of self-sacrifice for others; he did encourage little children to come to him, and recommend the childlike attitude. The Jesus who said, "Come to me, all of you who are tired from carrying your heavy loads, and I will give you rest" is a wonderful reality. But we gain nothing by suppressing the other, sterner aspect of the Jesus of the Gospels, the Jesus men were prepared to kill, and to die for, the Jesus who was sufficiently dynamic and controversial to start the most lasting revolution the world has seen.[9]

As Dr. France has adequately shown, it is possible to receive a distorted picture of Jesus today. It might not have to be a false picture, but merely an incomplete one. If disciples today are to be like disciples of the first century, they must keep examining the gospels with a fresh view and an open heart patterning their thoughts, words, and actions to that of the true Jesus. Jesus is the model for the disciple. The disciple is to be like Him because as the Father sent Him into the world, so He is sending the disciple. What Jesus taught, the disciple is to teach — "teaching them to observe all that I commanded you" (Matt. 28:20). The Apostle Peter summarizes the purpose of a disciple by stating that Christ gives us "an example that you should follow in His steps" (1 Peter 2:21).

## MARKS OF A DISCIPLE

### Abiding in the Word

There are three texts in the gospel of John that show the marks of a disciple. The first mark of a disciple is that He "abides in the Word." Jesus said, "If you abide in my word, then you are truly disciples of Mine" (John 8:31).

To abide in the word of Jesus meant that the disciple must persevere and continue to understand and comprehend His teaching. Much of Jesus' teaching was not readily comprehended. Often Jesus would have to take the disciples aside and teach them His meaning as He did after telling the Parable of the Sower in Matthew 13:10-23. Jesus asked them, "Have you understood all these things?" They said to Him, "Yes" (Matt. 13:51). Their affirmative answer did not in reality mean that they had grasped all of Jesus' truths as He wanted. Their answer might be parallel to the young boy who was listening to an adult Bible study. After it concluded, he was asked if he understood what was said. He replied, "I understand everything. I just don't know what it means." The disciples were similar to this young man. They understood Jesus to a point, but they were going to have to grow, listen more, and observe to a greater extent before they would truly comprehend the message.

For the disciples in the gospels, abiding in the Word meant that they would listen to what Jesus had to say as they were with Him. It was important not only to listen to His words but also to meditate on them and practice what He said in order that His word became a part of them. Jesus was the Word incarnate (John 1:1). As a result, abiding in the Word meant continuing with Him and being conformed to Him. Abiding in the Word could even be synonymous with Paul's terminology of "in Christ" (Romans 8:1).

The disciple who would continue to abide in the Word would not forsake or leave his Master. Some disciples were not willing to count the cost of following Jesus. After Jesus' discourse concerning His flesh and blood, many had second thoughts about continuing after Jesus. "As a result of this, many of His disciples withdrew, and were not walking with Him anymore" (John 6:66). A true disciple continued to abide in the Word of Jesus even when it was difficult to understand or difficult to obey. They did this because they trusted Him and were becoming like Him. "So then faith comes by hearing, and hearing by the word of Christ" (Romans 10:17).

Abiding in the Word is similar to a plant in the soil. A plant must abide in the soil and continually draw sustenance from the soil. The plant cannot live apart from the soil. Abiding is also like a fish in the water. In order for a fish to live, he must be abiding in the water drawing out oxygen for his gills.[10] If the fish is removed from his element, water, he will die. A disciple's element is the Word. He must continue in the Word as a fish continues in the water. If a disciple is removed from his element, the Word, he is like a fish out of water and will die.

Disciples today do not have the same privilege of verbalizing with Jesus as the disciples in the gospels did. However, this does not mean that there is a lack of communication. Jesus speaks to His disciple today through the Word, the Bible. A disciple of Jesus Christ today must abide in the Bible if he is to be communicating with Christ. A person cannot be a disciple if he does not know what His teacher says. A disciple is always learning from his teacher, and this relationship cannot develop unless the disciple listens to the teacher. As the early disciples listened to the words from Jesus' mouth, disciples today listen to the Bible.

The Bible is authoritative to the disciple. The Bible itself claims to be God's Word: "All scripture is God-breathed and is useful for teaching, rebuking, correcting, and training in righteousness, so that the man of God may be thoroughly equipped for every good work" (2 Timothy 3:16-17, NIV). The Bible is authoritative to the disciple today — just as Jesus' actual words were to those early disciples. The New Testament message is the Word of Christ for disciples today.

The disciple takes Jesus at His Word, and he believes it. If we were to reduce abiding to its least common denominator, it would mean simply to "obey."[11] Whatever He says, the disciples will obey. Even when the Word seems incomprehensible, the disciple follows because of his trust and obedience.

There are three things that are involved in abiding in the Word: one must receive it, he must contemplate it, and he must apply it.[12] The Word is received when it is read. A disciple should feed on the Word daily through a quiet time and also study it regularly. The Word of God is also received as the disciple hears it preached. A disciple will want to regularly hear the Word proclaimed because through the preaching of the Word more insight is gathered. Scripture memorization also is an important part of receiving the Word. By memorizing the Word, the message of God is always with the disciple and ready for recall.

Contemplating the Scripture is done by meditation. This involves thinking about the Word over and over again until concepts and truths actually become a part of this disciple. The Word is on the mind of the disciple to such a great extent that it becomes the mind set (Colossians 3:2). It is only through a steady contemplation of the Scriptures that the disciple obtains "the mind of Christ" (1 Corinthians 2:16). Because Jesus memorized the Scripture and meditated on it until it became a part of Him, He was able to think of God's Word and quote it when he faced temptation (Matthew 4:1-11).

The Scriptures must not only be received and contemplated, but they must also be applied. Jesus' message is one to be lived and practiced. The message of discipleship is a way of life. It can never stop with just some type of a mental exercise. As mentioned earlier, abiding implies obedience. As a result, the disciples must take the Word and make it become an integral part of his everyday life. "But prove yourselves doers of the Word, and not merely hearers who delude themselves" (James 1:22).

## Loving One Another

The second mark of a disciple was that they "loved one another." Jesus said: "A new commandment I give to you, that you love one another, even as I have loved you, that you also love one another. By this all men will know that you are My disciples, if you have love for one another" (John 13:34-35).

This statement by Jesus at first appears confusing because of the fact that He called it a new commandment. Why is it new? The Old Testament also called people to love — "you shall love your neighbor as yourself" (Leviticus 19:18), but Jesus' commandment indeed is different and new. It is new in three areas — object, measure, and purpose.

The commandment is new in object because the object of the love is the disciples. The disciples of Christ are to love each other. If Jesus had only discipled one person, He would not have taught this lesson. An individual disciple is limited in the way he reflects Christ to others. A disciple needs another disciple to experience fully the type of love Jesus wants him to know.

A disciple can and should love his neighbor who is a non-Christian, but this type of love is limited. A Christian and a non-Christian do not have the same purpose, priorities, and other things in common that two Christians have. They are following two different masters. As a result, the love of a disciple and a non-Christian never has the ability to reach the deepest level. If, then a disciple is to find love beyond the superficial level, he must encounter another disciple to love.

Jesus established the church because in His infinite wisdom He knew that believers would need each other. The ultimate love that can exist between human beings only exists in the body of Christ. For this reason, a disciple can never be an isolationist. He cannot be content with just a vertical, personal relationship with God. There must also be a healthy, horizontal relationship with brothers and sisters in Christ — "for the one who does not love his brother whom he has seen, cannot love God whom he has not seen" (1 John 4:20).

The commandment by Jesus in John 13:34-35 is also new in measure. In the Old Testament, the command was to love as you love yourself. Jesus' statement is much greater. He tells His disciples to love as He has loved — a new measure. Jesus had just demonstrated His selfless love to them by washing their feet, and He was calling them to similar service. Jesus' love was an unconditional love. It was like the rain that rains on the just and the unjust (Matthew 5:45). He loved not because people were so lovable, but because they were in so much need of love — "in that while we were yet sinners, Christ died for us" (Romans 5:8). His love was steadfast, and He held nothing back, not even his own life. The love of Christ was based more than just on feelings but on an uncompromising will to love people. Jesus was now calling his disciples to love by this measure.

The purpose of this commandment is also new. The purpose is an evangelistic one — so that all men will know that these are Jesus' disciples. Disciples of Christ should be able to be identified by non-Christians by the love that they demonstrate toward each other. The norm for most groups of humans is conflict and disharmony. The unity and love of Christians is strikingly different than that of the world and is a witness to non-Christians. Jesus prayed for this love and unity when he was in the Garden of Gethsemane because He knew people would not believe unless there was love among His disciples and the ones who would believe through their word.

> "I do not ask in behalf of these alone, but for those also who believe in Me through their word; that they may all be one; even as Thou, Father, art in Me, and I in Thee, that they also may be in Us; that the world may believe that Thou didst send Me" (John 17:20-21).

Loving one another is a foundational characteristic for disciples. As a result, a disciple must be a part of a church and displaying love toward his brothers and sisters in the congregation. It is this love for one another that attracts the non-believer to Christ and makes future discipleship possible. Too many Christians are critics, faultfinders, and gossips. This demeanor is the opposite of the unique love Jesus has called disciples to have. Jesus' disciples love one another.

## Bearing Fruit

The third mark of a disciple in the gospel of John was "fruit bearing." Jesus said, "By this is My Father glorified, that you bear much fruit, and so prove to be my disciples" (John 15:8). The proof of whether or not one is a disciple is if he bears fruit.

The key to bearing fruit is found in verse seven — abide. "If you abide in Me . . . and so prove to be my disciples" (John 15:7-8). The disciple must again be abiding in Jesus to bear fruit "for apart from Me you can do nothing" (John 15:5). The disciple must realize that he is totally dependent upon Jesus, and in and of himself, he can do nothing. But through abiding in Jesus, the disciple can bear much fruit.

What does it mean to "bear fruit"? One interpretation would be that this means evangelizing or winning people to Christ. This is what Paul means when he is writing to the Philippian church. "But if I am to live on in the flesh, this will mean fruitful labor for me" (Philippians 1:22). In this passage, Paul believes that if he is released from prison and was able to return to Philippi that he would win many more to Christ. Another interpretation of bearing fruit might be putting on the virtues that Paul called fruit of the Spirit. "But the fruit of the Spirit is love, joy, peace, patience, kindness, goodness, faithfulness, gentleness, self-control, against such things there is no law" (Galatians 5:22-23). One might choose this second interpretation to rationalize that bearing fruit is not evangelism. However, just because Paul uses "fruit" to mean one thing in his letters does not necessarily mean that it can be equated with Jesus' meaning in John 15.

To understand the meaning of "bearing fruit", the context of the chapter must be analyzed. There are three concepts that fit together in John 15. They are abiding in the Father's love, keeping His commandments, and bearing fruit. These three are like a three-legged stool. They all help support each other. When someone loves God, he keeps His commandments, and His commandments are not burdensome (1 John 5:3). When God's commandments are kept, the disciple bears fruit. This is what Jesus means in the Great Commission when he says, "teaching them to observe all that I commanded you" (Matthew 28:20). When one obeys and teaches all that Jesus commanded, he bears fruit. This includes not only a virtuous life but also making disciples of others because that is what they observed Jesus doing. As one bears fruit in his life, his love for God increases because he is filled with gratitude for the way God has changed his life and made him a fruit bearing disciple. His increased love makes him obey God's commandments more zealously which results in him bearing more fruit. The cycle goes on endlessly, but the end result is maturity. Maturity in Christ can never be achieved without fruit bearing. Donald Grey Barnhouse hits the mark when he said, "There are those who talk and who preach and who have multitudes of meetings, but there's no fruit. Activity is no substitute for fruit bearing!"[13]

Peter was asked the question, "you are not also one of this man's disciples, are you?" (John 18:17). This is a good question for all Christians to consider. How can one really tell if an affirmative answer would be genuine? Three things must be evident in the disciple's life: abiding in the Word, loving one another, and bearing fruit.

## QUESTIONS

1. How does a "disciple" differ from the modern usage of "pupil"?

2. What can you learn about discipleship from the Greek philopsophers that helps you understand what Jesus was doing?

3. How could we be practicing idolatry today and yet think we are Christians?

4. How can we get to know the real Jesus?

5. What misconceptions and distortions do people have about Jesus today?

6. What are the marks of a disciple given in the gospel of John? Explain each one of these.

7. What are you lacking in these three marks of a disciple?

## FOOTNOTES

1 K.H. Rengstorf, " μαθητής," *Theological Dictionary of the New Testament,* Vol. IV, ed. Gerhard Kittel, (Grand Rapids: Wm. B. Eerdmans, 1967), p. 416.

2 Rengstorf, p. 416.

3 Rengstorf, p. 417.

4 Keith Phillips, *The Making of a Disciple* (Old Tappan: Fleming H. Revell, 1981), p. 14.

5 Rengstorf, p. 420.

6 Phillips, p. 15.

7 Phillips, p. 15.

8 Thomas à Kempis, *Of the Imitation of Christ* (Springdale: Whitaker House, 1981), p. 11.

9 R.T. France, *I Came to Set the Earth on Fire* (Downers Grove: Inter-Varsity Press, 1975), pp. 13-14.

10 Gene Warr, *You Can Make Disciples* (Waco: Word Books, 1978), pp. 65-66.

11 Warr, p. 43.

12 Warr, p. 44.

13 Donald Grey Barnhouse, *The Love Life* (Glendale: Regal, 1973), p. 171.

# THE TASK
# OF THE
# DISCIPLE

3

## THE THREE E's

**I**f the biblical term, "disciple," is turned into a gerund, a new word is established which describes the task of the disciple. This word is "discipling." Discipling involves three things: evangelism, edification, and equipping.

### Evangelizing

Evangelism is the process of bringing one who is lost to a saved condition in Christ through the proclamation of the gospel. God is "not wanting any to perish, but everyone to come to repentance" (2 Peter 3:9, NIV). Realizing God's desire for all to be saved, a disciple tells the good news of God's saving grace in Christ Jesus to people who have not yet received Christ. Evangelism is what takes place when those who were lost change their allegiance to Christ and become converts. A good example of this takes place in Acts 2 when Peter proclaimed the message of Jesus' death, burial and resurrection to the crowd gathered there on the day of Pentecost.

The people there were cut to the heart upon hearing the gospel and wanted to know what to do to remedy their hopeless situation (Acts 2:37). Peter responded to them and told them to repent and be baptized (Acts 2:38). There were 3,000 upon that day that responded to the message and became converts. People giving their lives to Jesus and being converted is the goal of evangelism. As people receive the new birth, the evangel is accomplished.

Disciples today must be a part of the evangelism process. This means that a disciple goes into the world and shares his life (1 Thessalonians 2:8) and the gospel (Romans 1:16) with those who do not know Jesus. A disciple cannot divorce himself from the world, but must be in it winning souls to Jesus. Some may think that there is a higher calling than evangelism, but it is always fundamental for the disciple who conforms to his Master. Jesus' purpose was quite clear — "For the Son of Man came to seek and to save what was lost" (Luke 19:10, NIV).

Jesus called His disciples to be witnesses — "You will be my witnesses in Jerusalem, and in all Judea and Samaria, and to the ends of the earth" (Acts 1:8, NIV). Witnessing describes a way of life. A witness is not something you do as much as it is what you are. A witness does not have to go do evangelism because his entire lifestyle is evangelistic. Wherever he goes he puts in a good word for Jesus. All of his actions and words are a witness to the salvation that is in Jesus. A witness does not require an evangelism program or method because his entire motivation for living is to bring glory to God and people to Christ. Therefore, evangelism is as natural to him as breathing. Can one be a disciple and not be a witness? This would be like saying one can be a Christian and not be like Christ. Donald Grey Barnhouse makes this point clear:

> The moment a man becomes aware that he has been made alive in Christ, there is the urge to let someone else know about it. That urge is as natural as the cry of the newborn infant. When no such desire to witness occurs, there may be a serious question as to whether a stillbirth has taken place instead of the birth of a living healthy babe in Christ.[1]

*Edifying*

The second part of discipling is edification. This involves follow-up. When someone is born, he is a baby who cannot take care of himself. This is also true with the new birth. When someone is born again, he needs guidance and help to know what to do and what not to do. However, many new Christians do not receive the support, encouragement, and help they need. Some evangelistic programs concentrate to such an extent on bringing people to Christ that they neglect the new Christian after he is converted. If parents neglected their baby after birth the child would soon die. This is what happens too often in the spiritual realm when a new Christian is neglected and then dies spiritually. If parents treated their children like many Christians treat new converts, they would quickly be arrested for child neglect.

A new Christian needs teaching. Jesus included this in the Great Commission. The new life did not stop with baptism. The disciples were to teach all that Jesus had commanded them. New Christians need to know how to study the Word, how to pray, how to worship, and how to live daily for the Lord. They need to know basic doctrines about God, Jesus, the Holy Spirit, the church, salvation, and other important foundational beliefs. New Christians need to learn how to be a witness in the environments in which God has placed them. As a child needs to grow and mature, so does a new Christian. And the new believer will only grow as he is taught.

In the edification process, the marks of a disciple are built into a new convert's life. Edification is to bring the new Christian into maturity or "until Christ be formed in you" (Galatians 4:19). "So then, just as you have received Christ Jesus as Lord, continue to live in Him, rooted and built up in Him, strengthened in the faith as you were taught, and overflowing with thankfulness" (Colossians 2:6-7, NIV).

### Equipping

The third part of the task of the disciple is equipping. "And he gave some as apostles, and some as prophets, and some as evangelists, and some as pastors and teachers, for the equipping of the saints for the work of service, to the building up of the body of Christ" (Ephesians 4:11-12). This is the process where a disciple is led from being a convert to the point of his becoming a worker, one who is also reaping the harvest. The disciple is equipped so that he can now evangelize and edify other people. He is trained in order that he will become a spiritual leader who will reproduce himself in other people in the three areas of evangelism, edification and equipping.

Salvation and maturity are not all that Jesus wants in a disciple. He also desires that His disciples reproduce themselves. This was the strategy of Jesus — to reproduce Himself in the lives of others who would also reproduce. This is why He devoted so much of His time in the equipping of the twelve. He was going to send them out into the world (John 17:18), and they would go as the Father had sent Him (John 20:21). It becomes apparent that discipling not only involves people in the present generation but also people of future spiritual generations.

It is obvious that most churches today are not practicing the discipling process. Too many have just concentrated the ministry on the edification stage at the expense of the other two tasks. But a Christian cannot reach a full maturity in Christ if he is not reaching out to others in evangelism. And the church does not have a true leadership if it is not equipping others who will be discipling others. The area of equipping is probably the most neglected area of discipleship in churches today, and yet it was the most important in the ministry of Jesus.

The complete discipling process is very much like the

cycle of physical life. The first task (evangelism) is similar to the birth of a child. The second task (edification) is analogous to the raising of the child. Equipping, the third task, relates to the sending out of the person who is now mature enough to reproduce and raise others.[2] All of these tasks are vital to discipleship, and they must all be present and working together if Christians today are to have discipleship ministries.

## REPRODUCE AFTER OWN KIND

No one likes a hypocrite, and nothing hinders the growth of the church more than someone who says one thing and does another. Nearly everyone identifies or thinks of someone when they read the following poem by Edgar Guest:

I'd rather see a sermon than hear one any day.
  I'd rather one should walk with me than merely show
    the way.
The eye's a better pupil and more willing than the ear;
  Fine counsel is confusing, but example's always clear;
And the best of all the preachers are the men who live
  their creeds,
  For to see the good in action is what everybody needs.
I can soon learn how to do it, if you'll let me see it done.
  I can watch your hands in action, but your tongue too
    fast may run.
And the lectures you deliver may be very wise and true,
  but I'd rather get my lesson by observing what you do.
For I may misunderstand you and the high advice you
  give,
  but there's no misunderstanding how you act and how
    you live.[3]

Most Christians have been guilty of saying, "Do what I say and not what I do." An individual might hear that cliche, "You are the only Bible some people will ever read," and all of a sudden, Christianity becomes scary to the follower of Christ. A believer can develop a spiritual paranoia because he knows that he is not the example that he ought to be. Example is the primary way one trains disciples. If one becomes a follower of the Lord Jesus Christ, one's life will always be open for examination. People will be watching and patterning their lives after what they see.

An important spiritual principle is once again found in the physical realm. In the creation of the various animals of the world, an important biological fact is ascertained.

> Then God said, 'Let the earth bring forth living creatures after their kind; cattle and creeping things and beasts of the earth after their kind;' and it was so. And God made the beasts of the earth after their kind, and the cattle after their kind, and every thing that creeps on the ground after its kind; and God saw that it was good" (Genesis 1:24-25).

This same principle of reproduction after one's own kind holds true in the area of disciplemaking. The fact of the matter is that one reproduces after his own kind whether he likes it or not. This is one of the most sobering truths in the Bible.

Most Christians would be hesitant to say today, "Be followers of me." To make such a statement would be considered among some to be blasphemous. And yet, the apostle Paul made statements like this one: "I exhort you therefore, be imitators of me" (1 Corinthians 4:16). "Be imitators of me, just as I also am of Christ" (1 Corinthians 11:1). The Hebrew writer teaches Christians to imitate their leaders. "Remember those who led you, who spoke the Word of God to you; and considering the outcome of their way of life, imitate their faith" (Hebrews 13:7). Believers today are saying, "Paul may have been able to say that, but I could certainly never say that. Don't follow me. Follow Jesus Christ." But the fact of the matter is that disciples will follow their leader whether the leader wants them to or not. A leader can say, "Be this way," but the disciple will probably be like the leader.

If a disciple maker cannot say, "Be followers of me," then there is something drastically wrong with his life. Do leaders have to be perfect in order to disciple? No, but they must be striving for perfection, and when they do sin, they set an example of coming to the cross with their sin. If someone is striving for perfection, being conformed to the image of Christ, and taking all of his sins to the cross; then his life truly can be imitated.

When a disciple maker begins to help a person in the Christian life, he will follow his leader as naturally as a young child follows his parents. And it is more than probable that the new disciple will imitate what the teacher does rather than following just what he says. A church leader may preach repeatedly that Christians ought to be evangelistic but unless he himself is winning souls to Jesus, the possibilities are very remote that the people whom he disciples will be evangelistic. Keith Phillips expresses the concept concisely:

> Most of who we are today is a result of watching and listening to others. We learned how to talk by imitating our parents and other children in school. We formed personal preferences about dress, recreation, music and entertainment by copying the likes and dislikes of our family and peers. Even our thinking and philosophy of life were greatly influenced by those around us.
>
> Making a disciple is a process that begins with being a model. Character is caught, not taught.[4]

The Scriptures bear this out, that one reproduces after his own kind. Abraham had a tremendous love for Isaac, the son of the promise. He probably had great expectations for him to grow up and be a godly man who would not make the same mistakes that his father had made. In Genesis 20:1-7, Abraham deceived Abimelech by telling him that his wife, Sarah, was really his sister. He did this out of fear and in order to save his own life. But the action was still wrong because he was deceptive. Abraham would have wanted Isaac to never follow this example, but he did. "When the men of the place asked about his wife, he said, 'She is my sister,' for he was afraid to say, 'my wife,' thinking, 'the men of the place might kill me on account of Rebekah, for she is beautiful" (Genesis 26:7). Abraham reproduced after his own kind. His actions had spoken louder than his words.

Another example is Eli, the great spiritual leader of Israel. Eli teaches a lot about discipleship by the way he devoted his time to training his successor, Samuel. Eli trained Samuel well but must have neglected the spirituality of his own family. He did a poor job of raising his sons. "Now the sons of Eli were worthless men; they did not know the Lord" (1 Samuel 2:12). Eli's sons, Hophni and Phinehas, selfishly acquired more of the sacrifices than was their priestly due and turned the people away from the offering of the Lord. Even though Eli trained Samuel well, his example of a bad family life was reproduced in his protege. "And it came about when Samuel was old that he appointed his sons judges over Israel . . . . His sons, however, did not walk in his ways, but turned aside after dishonest gain and took bribes and perverted justice" (1 Samuel 8:1-2). Again, the principle is seen as Eli reproduced after his own kind.

Conversely, a good example which is reproduced is found in Jesus and his close disciples. Jesus was the perfect model for them. "For I gave you an example that you also should do as I did to you" (John 13:15). They would make disciples not merely because they knew Jesus but because they had become like Him. Jesus' disciples had observed him and been with Him in all types of life situations. They had eaten with Him, they heard Him preach, they saw Him perform miracles, and they saw Him relate to people from all walks of life. And if they did not understand everything, He began "explaining everything privately to His own disciples" (Mark 4:34).

The disciples' lives were transformed by Jesus. They would never be able to forget all that they had seen and heard. The message that they proclaimed was what they had witnessed. "That which was from the beginning, which we have heard, which we have seen with our eyes, which we have looked at and our hands have touched — this we proclaim concerning the Word of Life" (1 John 1:1). If the disciples had copied a lesser model, their results would have been of far less magnitude.

As Christ was the ideal model for His disciples, disciples today need to be examples for those whom they are training. A wise old mountaineer spoke, "You can't give what you ain't got any more than you can come from where you ain't been."[5] Jesus said, "For men do not gather figs from thorns, nor do they pick grapes from a briar bush" (Luke 6:44). "Iron sharpens iron, so one man sharpens another" (Proverbs 27:17).

It is imperative in discipleship to major on being the kind of person that it would be desirous for the disciple to become. Paul taught Timothy this lesson: "Pay close attention to yourself and to your teaching; persevere in these things; for as you do this you will insure salvation both for yourself and for those who hear you" (1 Timothy 4:16). In this passage, Paul explains two things that are of utmost importance to everyone: the salvation of one's self and the salvation of others. If then one wants to be saved and desires others to be saved, he must pay close attention to these two aspects: his example and the doctrine that he teaches. The instruction here conveys that if one wants to be saved, he must know the truth and be conformed to the Master. And the only hope for someone else to be discipled is to hear the truth and see Jesus living in a person.

A disciple maker must then ask himself, "What kind of a disciple will a person be if he imitates my example?" A disciple maker can be certain that he will reproduce the qualities that he has in his own life whether they are good or bad. If the disciple maker looks out to his disciples and beholds things that he does not like, he must look into the mirror first. If he suspects that the elements of a disciple are not in his own life, he must go back to the fundamentals in his own life. A disciple will reproduce after his own kind. A good example of this is illustrated in

37

Paul's ministry in Thessalonica. "You know how we lived among you for your sake. You became imitators of us and of the Lord" (1 Thessalonians 1:5-6, NIV).

There are many reasons why an example is valuable to a disciple: (1) an example gives one a pattern for a change in behavior, (2) when one sees someone else, he believes that it is possible, (3) we learn to imitate the Lord by imitating an example, (4) being an example gives credibility, and (5) an example encourages the disciple to do things that he was formerly afraid of doing.

When it is all boiled down, those of us who are seeking to train men must be prepared to have them follow us, even as we follow Christ (1 Cor. 11:1). We are the exhibit (Phil. 3:17f.; 1 Thess. 2:7,8; 2 Tim. 1:13). They will do those things which they hear and see in us (Phil. 4:9). Given time, it is possible through this kind of leadership to impart our way of living to those who are constantly with us.

We must take this truth to our lives. There can be no shirking or evading our personal responsibility to show the way to those we are training, and this revelation must include the practical outworking in life of the deeper realities of the Spirit. This is the Master's method, and nothing else will suffice to train others to do His work.[6]

## QUESTIONS

1. What are the three E's in the task of a disciple?
2. What are the differences between evangelism, edification, and equipping?
3. In which of these three is your church strongest? weakest?
4. In which of these three are you strongest? weakest?
5. Could you make the statement, "Be followers of me"? Why or why not?
6. What kind of life does a person need to have in order to have a life that can be imitated?

7. What are some biblical examples of reproducing after your own kind?

8. What two things should be of the utmost importance to everyone?

9. Why are examples important?

10. What changes do you need to make in your life to be a better example?

## FOOTNOTES

[1] Donald Grey Barnhouse, *The Love Life* (Glendale: Regal, 1973), p. 11.

[2] Allen Hadidian, *Successful Discipling* (Chicago: Moody Press, 1979), p. 22.

[3] Edgar Guest, *Collected Verses of E.A. Guest* (Chicago: Reilly and Lee, 1934), p. 509.

[4] Keith Phillips, *The Making of a Disciple* (Old Tappan: Fleming H. Revell, 1981), p. 148.

[5] Urie Bender, The Witness (Scottdale: Herald, 1965), p. 45.

[6] Robert Coleman, *The Master Plan of Evangelism,* (Old Tappan: Fleming H. Revell, 1963), p. 81.

# THE MULTIPLYING MINISTRY

4

## GEOMETRIC
## VERSUS ARITHMETIC PROGRESSION

C hristians often picture evangelism as the world versus them and because there is an overwhelmingly greater number in the world than in the church, world evangelism is too often seen as hopeless. Perhaps the real problem is that Christians have not understood properly Jesus' plan for a multiplying ministry.

In 1980 the world population was approximately 4.5 billion. As an example, suppose a preacher of a five hundred member congregation decided that he ought to be involved in world evangelization. He realizes that he is speaking each week to predominately the same people. As a result, he sets up a plan to reach the world for Christ. He decides that he will preach to groups of five hundred different people every day until he speaks to everyone in the world. As a result, an advance team is organized that goes before him assembling people together all over the world in order that there is a new group of 500 people for him to tell about Jesus every day. If everyone did their part, these groups were assembled, and five hundred different people heard the gospel every day; it would take only 24,658 years for the evangelistic team to teach the gospel one time to the people of the world. This would also be assuming that the group took no vacations or days off and that the world experienced no population growth. At the onset, this sounded like a good plan, but when it is examined fully, it leaves one only frustrated again with the problem of world evangelization.

As an alternative strategy, suppose this minister shares Jesus with his friends, relatives, associates, and neighbors. In the process of sharing his faith, he selects three individuals who demonstrate a willingness to know, love, and glorify Jesus. After these three are evangelized, he works with them in order that they might be brought to maturity. The minister spends time with them in all types of situations. He teaches them how to worship, how to study the Bible, and how to pray. They learn the importance of the church and basic biblical doctrine. He goes with them and demonstrates how to be a witness for Jesus in the world and then sends them out to do it themselves. These three are instilled with a world vision and acquire a burden for the lost. If this minister gave these three people the priority time in his ministry for one year and equipped them that year to such an extent that each one could train three others the next year who could also reproduce, the results would be staggering.

Table #1 demonstrates what would happen in such a ministry.

It becomes apparent that after only seventeen years with this method of ministry, every one in the world could be reached even with population growth. It is true that not everyone will accept Christ which makes this illustration idealistic. It is also true that God may not choose to work in little groups of three with everyone. But the point is — if Christians want to win the world to Christ, this is the method. Christians can only reach the masses if they are part of a plan that multiplies the workers.

## Table #1

### Geometric Progression of a
### Multiplying Ministry

| | |
|---|---|
| Year 1 | 4 disciples |
| Year 2 | 16 disciples |
| Year 3 | 64 disciples |
| Year 4 | 256 disciples |
| Year 5 | 1,024 disciples |
| Year 6 | 4,096 disciples |
| Year 7 | 16,384 disciples |
| Year 8 | 65,536 disciples |
| Year 9 | 262,144 disciples |
| Year 10 | 1,048,576 disciples |
| Year 11 | 4,194,304 disciples |
| Year 12 | 16,777,216 disciples |
| Year 13 | 67,108,864 disciples |
| Year 14 | 268,435,456 disciples |
| Year 15 | 1,073,741,284 disciples |
| Year 16 | 4,294,967,196 disciples |
| Year 17 | 17,179,869,184 disciples |

One Sunday evening during an assembly, I asked various individuals, one at a time, to stand. After a few minutes, there were about 15 people standing. Later I asked a few individuals to stand and asked them to ask others to do the same with others and others with others; in the same amount of time it had taken me to ask fifteen people to stand, the entire assembly of four hundred was on their feet. This illustration demonstrates the problem with evangelism. In the first illustration, all of the people who were standing were dependent upon one person asking them to stand, the minister. This is the way evangelism occurs in too many churches. It is dependent solely upon the minister. People who are brought to Christ become converts because the minister converted them. If only the minister is bringing people to the Lord, the results are minimal. On the other hand, if everyone gets into the picture as in the second illustration, the effect can be phenomenal. When others were asking others to stand, it did not take long for everyone to stand. Similarly, when everyone is bringing people to the Lord and these people are bringing others, it does not take long to reach many people. If churches are to take world evangelization seriously, it will only happen when everyone gets involved and not just the minister.

Alvin Jennings believes that in many churches, it may be "the preacher" who is the only one reaching out and converting the lost. He explains that "the moment he relaxes, the growth levels off or begins to decline. He has failed in half of his ministry. Even Jesus would have failed had He not trained faithful men to be teachers of what He taught them."[1]

Disciples are to made geometrically rather than arithmetically. Arithmetical progression is where a series of numbers increase or decrease by a common difference. Arithmetical progression could be demonstrated by numbers increasing by two, e.g. 2, 4, 6, 8, 10, 12. This is the type of increase that resulted when the minister decided to preach to groups of five hundred around the world. It is also the type of progression that resulted when only the minister asked people to stand. Arithmetical progression shows a definite and consistent increase, but its growth rate is far less dramatic than geometric progression.

Geometric progression is when there is a series of quantities in which each quantity is obtained by multiplying the preceding number by a constant factor. Geometric progression could be demonstrated with three being a constant factor, e.g. 2, 6, 18, 54. Geometric progression multiplies instead of adding. When the minister entrusted his faith to those three people in the illustration, a good example of geometric progression resulted. When everyone was asking everyone else to stand up in the illustration, the multiplying factor came into effect. Jesus' way of bringing the world to Him is through geometric progression. Disciples are to multiply. When disciples can comprehend the power of a multiplying ministry, the possibility of the Great Commission quickly becomes more conceivable.

If churches are to be fulfilling the Great Commission, then a top priority must be to multiply the workers. John Raleigh Mott rightly summarized the task by saying: "Greater is he that multiplies the workers than he who does the work." This was a paraphrase of Samuel Morley's philosophy: "He who does the work is not so profitably employed as he who multiplies the doers." Dwight L. Moody put it this way: "It's better to put ten men to work than to do the work of ten men."[2]

## A FACT OF NATURE

The multiplication process may seem to be new in our thinking for church growth, but in reality it is a very old fact of nature.

"And God blessed them; and God said to them, 'Be fruitful and multiply and fill the earth, and subdue it; and rule over the fish of the sea and over the birds of the sky, and over every living thing that moves on the earth" (Genesis 1:28).

When the commandment to multiply was first given, there were only two human beings, Adam and Eve. It is obvious by looking at the world today that the principle of multiplication works because those two people have multiplied into around 4.5 billion people. If people have obeyed any commandment of God, this is one that they have done a good job in obeying.

Dr. Jerry White, formerly an instructor in astronautics at the United States Air Force Academy, produced a demonstration that serves as yet another illustration of the power of multiplication. Dr. White posed the experiment of folding fifty times a piece of thin india paper, the thickness of a page in the Bible. Using a computer, he found that if that piece of paper could be folded in half fifty times, it would be seventeen million

45

miles long. This would be a distance equivalent to going to the moon and back thirty-four times.[3]

The Museum of Science and Industry in Chicago demonstrated this fact of nature with the use of a checkerboard. On one square of the checkerboard was one grain of wheat, on the second square were two grains of wheat, on the third was four, then eight, and the process kept doubling until there were so many grains of wheat on one square that they were piling onto other squares. The Museum asked, "At this rate of doubling every square, how much grain would you have on the checkerboard by the time you reached the 64th square?" The surprising answer to this display was "Enough to cover the entire subcontinent of India 50 feet deep."[4]

In the field of finance, what would be better: to receive a salary of two thousand dollars per month or a penny a day doubled each day? A penny a day that is doubled appears to be very cheap wages. Wages of a penny the first day, two cents the second, and four cents the third does not seem like very much. However, after only thirty-one days, this salary would equal over twenty million dollars — not a bad month's wage.

The point of these illustrations is that nature has shown that multiplication works and is the fastest method to reach the world. Jesus employed this principle as His plan of bringing the world to Him. The process starts off more slowly than others but catches up and surpasses other growth processes after a short time.

In today's modern age, society wants things instantly. As a result, people today tend to opt for mass production more than quality workmanship. Some churches today are so anxious for results and a drastic increase in numbers that they are not willing to wait for disciples to multiply. These churches will try many types of quick evangelistic methods but because of their lack of patience and failure to make disciples, they will have not only fewer people but also people with less maturity.

Making disciples in the multiplying fashion not only insures a greater number in the long run but also gives quality control.

Since life is so short for an individual and the gospel message is so urgent, the necessity for an outreach that multiplies becomes an imperative. Everyone wants their life to count for something — something that is lasting. Anyone who is a part of a multiplying discipleship has committed his life to something that counts, and it counts for eternity.

## QUESTIONS

1. Which one of the methods of growth was more appealing to you — the one teaching 500 a day or the one which equips three a year? Why?

2. Is everyone involved in evangelism in your church or only the minister?

3. What is the difference between geometric and arithmetic progression?

4. What is a plan of action that we could do in the church to multiply the workers?

5. What are some examples from nature that demonstrate this multiplying factor?

6. Why is it so important to have a plan that multiplies the worker?

## FOOTNOTES

[1] Alvin Jennings, 3 R's of Urban Church Growth (Fort Worth: Star, 1981), p. 81.

[2] Oscar E. Feucht, Everyone a Minister (St. Louis: Concordia, 1974), p. 146.

[3] Leroy Eims, The Lost Art of Disciple Making (Grand Rapids: Zondervan, 1978), p. 85.

[4] Walter Henrichsen, Disciples Are Made — Not Born (Wheaton: Victor, 1974), p. 143.

# MULTIPLICATION IN THE NEW TESTAMENT 5

## THE MULTIPLYING VERSE

**W**hen asked if leading a person to Christ was the greatest joy in life, Leroy Eims replied that there is something even greater than that. What is it that could be greater than seeing someone come to the Lord? He said, "When the person you have led to Christ grows and develops into a dedicated, fruitful, mature disciple who then goes on to lead others to Christ and helps them in turn as well."[1]

If a disciple wants to multiply, he must realize this truth of which Leroy Eims speaks. Disciples must look beyond the immediate converts. People who have been led to Christ by a disciple might be referred to as the second generation disciple. But if the disciple is to multiply, he must see the second generation disciple reproduce to at least a third generation. Seeing one's disciple reproduce to another generation as opposed to just him coming to the Lord is the difference in multiplying discipleship and mere evangelism. The multiplying effect that reaches a third generation and beyond occurs because in addition to evangelism, there is edification and equipping.

The following illustration demonstrates the multiplying effect of discipleship as seen in a third spiritual generation. The top level person represents a person who is committed to a multiplying ministry. The second level represents his disciples who have been equipped and will reproduce disciples in a third spiritual generation (the third level).[2]

**First Generation**

**Second Generation**

**Third Generation**

## Illustration #1
### Three Generations in Multiplying Discipleship

Paul, as he was writing his last letter to his disciple, wanted to be assured that Timothy understood this concept of multiplying disciples. His charge to Timothy is probably the most extensive statement on multiplying discipleship in the New Testament. "And the things you have heard me say in the presence of many witnesses entrust to reliable men who will also be qualified to teach others" (2 Timothy 2:2, NIV).

In this passage, Paul instructs that close brother whom he had discipled to disciple others in a similar manner. Paul is teaching him to have a third generation vision. When Paul mentions "the things you have heard me say," Timothy could reflect back on his experiences with Paul and recall a tremendous amount of teachings. He would be able to remember that day that he first heard Paul preach the gospel in Lystra. Perhaps Paul had a personal study with Timothy which led him to the Lord. Timothy would be able to reflect on the teaching that Paul taught to establish and ground the church in Lystra. He also learned a lot from him as he observed Paul being persecuted and stoned. He knew from Paul that following the Lord was serious business. It is also possible that Timothy was a member of one of the first churches to receive the Galatian letter. Timothy also had the privilege of traveling with Paul on missionary journeys. He must have learned daily how to cope and minister in all types of situations as he was a constant traveling companion. During their travels, Timothy would have been able to learn more fully how to pray, how to study God's Word, and how to teach others. Timothy was able to grow to an even greater extent as Paul sent him out and delegated responsibilities to him. Not only did Paul send him to other cities, but he also wrote letters to him. As a result, when Timothy thought of "the things you heard me say," it was an abundance of rich teaching concerning all facets of the Christian life.

When Paul told Timothy to "entrust" these things, perhaps Timothy recalled Jesus' parable of the talents where the Master entrusted a sum of money to His servants to be used fruitfully and to be increased. To entrust implies one person giving something to another. It manifests a commitment and a trust. What is he entrusting? All of the things mentioned earlier and more — his life. "Having thus a fond affection for you, we were pleased to impart to you not only the gospel of God, but also our own lives, because you had become very dear to us" (1 Thessalonians 2:8). Timothy was Paul's disciple. He was now to commit this relationship that they had to someone else. As Paul had invested his life in Timothy, Timothy was to invest his life in another disciple. Timothy had become like Paul as Paul had become like Christ. Everyone imitates those with whom they associate, and disciple makers reproduce after their own kind. Paul had reproduced after his own kind in Timothy. Now another was to become like Timothy as he had become like Paul as he had become like Christ.

Because of their association and the discipling process, Paul and Timothy must have become very much alike. Obviously, from the New Testament accounts, they have different personalities and backgrounds. Paul is bold; Timothy is timid. Paul is from the city; Timothy is from the small town. Paul has the wisdom of years; Timothy is young. Paul has a great Jewish heritage and training; Timothy is half-Greek from a city without a synagogue. Only God would make a team of two such unlikely individuals.

Even with all these differences, Timothy must have been just like Paul in many ways. If one asked Paul or Timothy a question on doctrine, the answers would have probably been the same. Their philosophy of ministry and lifestyle was probably very similar. Paul wrote to Timothy, "But you followed my teaching, conduct, purpose, faith, patience, love, perseverance, persecutions, sufferings" (2 Timothy 3:10-11). It was all of these things which composed Paul's life which had been entrusted to Timothy and was now to be entrusted to someone else.

To whom was all of this to be entrusted? Here lies the key — reliable men. Discipleship cannot occur unless one can find a reliable or faithful person. "Many a man claims to have unfailing love, but a faithful man who can find?" (Proverbs 20:6, NIV). There are many who may call themselves, "Christian," but they do not have the reliability to become multiplying disciples. Timothy was to be seeking out people to disciple who had already proven themselves to be reliable. God is looking for faithful people. "For the eyes of the Lord move to and fro throughout the earth that He may strongly support those whose heart is completely His" (2 Chronicles 16:9).

Paul concludes his charge by stating, "who will be able to teach others also." Now, Paul is talking about multiplication. In this passage, not only is a third spiritual generation seen but also a fourth. Paul (first generation) entrusts his faith to Timothy (second generation) who is told to commit his life to reliable men (third generation) who will be able to teach others (fourth generation) also. The following illustration (page 54) depicts these generations.

In this passage it becomes apparent how disciples are multiplied because only a part of the picture is seen. Timothy was not the only one Paul discipled. When Timothy departed to fulfill his ministry, Paul naturally discipled others who would disciple others. When Timothy's reliable men were teaching others, Timothy would be training more reliable men. The process was never to stop but to continue at a geometric progression. This was a multiplicative process that was to win the world to Christ and must be imitated in churches today. "Activity is no substitute for reproduction."[3]

## JESUS, THE FIRST EXAMPLE

Where did the apostle Paul come up with such a good plan? He was simply imitating his Master, Jesus. Jesus was the one who was the master of multiplication. His

**First Generation**  **Paul**

**Second Generation**  **Timothy**

**Third Generation** 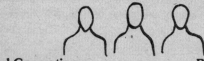 **Reliable Men**

**Fourth Generation**  **Others**

Illustration #2
The Multiplying Effect of Timothy 2:2

entire ministry was founded upon the strategy of multiplying a few men who would become like Him.

At the foundation of His ministry were a few people whom Jesus discipled. The multiplication of those trained men has already been examined, and this is exactly what Jesus did. Jesus especially devoted Himself to three men — Peter, James, and John. These three men became the great leaders in the early church.

Jesus reached out to the multitudes and crowds, but more than that he trained His twelve and the three. When the time of His death came, the crowds would forsake Jesus. Many had misunderstood Him, and others simply didn't want to pay the price to follow Him. But when the Spirit came on the day of Pentecost after His resurrection, Jesus' plan to reach the world depended upon whether or not these closest disciples were trained.

How were the twelve and the three trained? First of all, Jesus called them to follow Him and go with Him as He traveled throughout the land. As they followed Him, they listened to Him when He taught the multitudes and debated the scribes and Pharisees. Often times Jesus would get with them and explain in detail about His teaching. These disciples were there and observed Jesus as He performed various miracles. They spent time with Him in all types of situations. He also sent them out to teach and do miracles as He had done. They then reported back to Him, and He advised them further. Jesus' ministry had these men as a focal point. Although Jesus spent time with multitudes (those who opposed Him, and other groups), these disciples were always with Him. They were able to observe and emulate Jesus' life in every aspect. And upon that day of Pentecost, they were ready.

When Jesus told His disciples to "go and make disciples," He also said, "teaching them to observe all that I have commanded you." Included in this statement would be that the disciples were to teach to go and make disciples as they were taught to go and make disciples. The Great Commission is filled with the multiplication principle.

Jesus made disciples of these men, and they would make disciples of others who would do the same. The discipling of Peter, James, and John and the multiplication factor that resulted from it can be seen in the following illustration.

**Illustration #3**
**Jesus' Example of Multiplication**

Paul's statement, "Be imitators of me, just as I also am of Christ" (1 Corinthians 11:1), was indeed valid when it came to the matter of a multiplying ministry. In Paul's ministry a similar diagram could be used to characterize his ministry as was done with Jesus. All that needs to be changed are the names. Instead of Peter, James, and John; Timothy, Luke, and Titus, could be substituted.

**Illustration #4**
**Paul's Example of Multiplication**

# FOLLOWING THE LEADER

The pattern of multiplying Jesus was the plan for New Testament evangelism. Early Christians (in addition to Paul) devoted themselves to following Jesus' example of making disciples. The church was established in 30 A.D., and by the time of Paul's Colossian letter (about 30 years later), the gospel had gone into all the world (Colossians 1:6). How could the gospel go into all the world in just thirty years in an age without our modern communication systems? It could have only happened because disciples were multiplying.

How Paul had a multiplying ministry has been discussed. Indeed, his ministry was patterned after that of Jesus, but Paul also had the ability to see discipling take place first hand. It is often forgotten that Paul was discipled by one of the master disciplers, Barnabas. Barnabas also followed after the leader, Jesus, in his discipling approach. When Jesus chose His disciples, He chose some unlikely prospects — unlearned fishermen, a tax collector, and a Zealot to name a few. Barnabas, the Son of Encouragement, lived up to his name by seeing the possibilities in Paul. No one had the vision for what Paul could become with the exception of Barnabas:

"And when he had come to Jerusalem he was trying to associate with the disciples; and they were all afraid of him, not believing that he was a disciple. But Barnabas took hold of him and brought him to the apostles and described to them how he had seen the Lord on the road, and that He had talked to him, and how at Damascus he had spoken out boldly in the name of Jesus" (Acts 9:26-27).

Barnabas must have taught Paul many things in those early years of Paul's ministry, and he also discipled him as he went with him to send the contributions to Jerusalem (Acts 11:29-30), and as he accompanied Paul on the first missionary journey. Paul would probably have never learned to be the great spiritual leader who reached thousands if he had not been discipled by Barnabas.

Barnabas also discipled another important person. Barnabas had the tenacity to stick with the people when no one else would. On the first missionary journey, Barnabas leads out with two of his disciples — Paul and John Mark, his cousin. For some unknown reason, John Mark leaves the first journey. When Paul and Barnabas are about to go on the second missionary journey, Barnabas wants to take John Mark, but Paul refuses to take him. Barnabas, however, does not give up on John Mark and takes him along with him, parting company with Paul. Perhaps Barnabas knew that Paul could make it without him but John Mark still needed some discipling. It was to everyone's advantage that John Mark was discipled since he later pens the powerful gospel story. Only God knows how many people have been reached by the Gospel of Mark. He would not have been ready to write it if it had not been for Barnabas. John Mark also became an important help in Paul's ministry. "Pick up Mark and bring him with you, for he is useful to me for service" (2 Timothy 4:11).

Another example of the multiplying ministry can be seen in what happened in Thessalonica. Paul, Silas, and Timothy go to Thessalonica on the second missionary journey to establish a church there (1 Thessalonians 1:1). Many of the Thessalonians believed the message of Jesus which these three spoke. The faith of Paul, Silas, and Timothy was reproduced in the church there. "You also became imitators of us and of the Lord" (1 Thessalonians 1:6). In this passage it is seen how the Thessalonians imitate these three and become like the one Paul, Silas, and Timothy are imitating — the Lord Jesus Christ. But the reproduction does not stop there. The Thessalonians "became an example to all the believers in Macedonia and Achaia" (1 Thessalonians 1:7). However, the multiplication still has not come to an end. "For the word of the Lord has sounded forth from you, not only in Macedonia and Achaia, but also in every place your faith toward God has gone forth" (1 Thessalonians 1:8). Several spiritual generations can be seen in Thessalonica — Paul, Silas, and Timothy (first generation); the church in Thessalonica (second generation); and the believers in Macedonia and Achaia (third generation); and the believers in every place (fourth generation). The following illustration portrays this multiplication.

**Paul**  **Silas**  **Timothy**

**First Generation**

**Second Generation — Church in Thessalonica**

**Third Generation — Believers in Macedonia and Achaia**

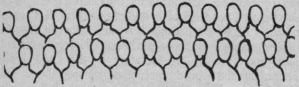

**Fourth Generation — Believers in Every Place**

**Illustration #5**
**The Multiplication of Disciples in Thessalonica**

A similar multiplication can be seen in Paul's ministry in Ephesus at the School of Tyrannus. After two years on the Tyrannus campus, "all who lived in Asia heard the word of the Lord, both Jews and Greeks" (Acts 19:10). How did this happen in two years when Paul was in one location? Similar to a university today, students from all over Asia must have come to learn at the School of Tyrannus. During their time at the school, they were discipled by Paul. Most students stay at a school for just a few years, and then they go back to their home towns or other places. Evidently, this is what happened in Ephesus. The people who were discipled at the School of Tyrannus left the school and took the Word throughout all Asia. As a result, Jews and Gentiles all over Asia heard about Jesus — another example of spiritual multiplication. (See illustration: *The Multiplication of Disciples in Ephesus*).

**Paul**

**School of Tyrannus**

**All Who Lived in Asia**

**Illustration #6**
**The Multiplication of Disciples in Ephesus**

It is interesting to combine Matthew 28:18-20 and Acts 8:26-39 to see another picture of multiplication. Jesus told his disciples to go and make disciples. His disciples convert and disciple Philip who led the Ethiopian eunuch to Christ. Tradition tells us that the Ethiopian eunuch was responsible for establishing the church in Africa. In this example, five generations can be seen: (1) Jesus, (2) the disciples, (3) Philip, (4) the Ethiopian eunuch, (5) Africans. Illustration , *The Multiplication of Disciples in Africa* displays this reproduction.

## A FEW GOOD MEN

The United States Marines have advertised that they are looking for a "few good men." Their strategy is that they can be more effective with a few specially trained and equipped men than they can with many who are not. The same principle applies to Jesus' plan of making disciples. Considering the plan for multiplication, a few good men can be infinitely more effective than many who are not truly disciples.

Churches today are constantly seeking new programs. Anyone who has a new idea concerning a method for growth could hold a seminar and probably many would come. But ultimately churches are going to have to go back to the New Testament and realize the method of Jesus. What is the method of Jesus? To put it quite simply, men were His method.

It all started by Jesus calling a few men to follow Him. This revealed immediately the direction His evangelistic strategy would take. His concern was not with programs to reach the multitudes, but with men whom the multitudes would follow. Remarkable as it may seem, Jesus started to gather these men before He ever organized an evangelistic campaign or even preached a sermon in public. Men were to be his method of winning the world to God.[4]

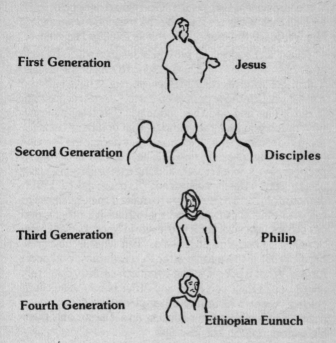

**First Generation** — Jesus

**Second Generation** — Disciples

**Third Generation** — Philip

**Fourth Generation** — Ethiopian Eunuch

**Fifth Generation** — Africa

Illustration #7
The Multiplication of Disciples in Africa

It seems preposterous that God would depend on men with all their weaknesses to be the method for spreading His will to all the world, but this is exactly His plan.

There is the story about when Jesus went to heaven after His ascension and was talking to one of the angels. The angel asked Jesus: "Master, you must have suffered a great deal for those people on earth." Jesus responded, "I did." The angel further inquired, "Do they all know how much you love them and all that you have done for them?" Jesus replied, "No, only a few people in Palestine know at this present time." The curious angel again probed: "Well, what have you done to let everyone know about you?" Jesus answered: "I have asked Peter, James, John and a few others to make it their business to tell everyone about me, and the others tell others, and yet others until everyone in the world knows what I have done." The doubtful angel said: "But what if they grow tired? What if the people after Peter, James, and John forget? What if people in the twentieth century don't talk about you? Don't you have any other plan?" Jesus concluded: "I don't have any other plans. I'm counting on them."[5] This is the plan of Jesus, and it is the only plan. He is counting on His disciples.

If His plan seems unbelievable because men are the method, it becomes even more difficult to grasp when it is realized that it begins with just a few men. Jesus never neglected the masses or the multitudes, but His concentration was upon a few, the twelve and especially Peter, James and John. Churches today are often so anxious to see and reach the masses that a proper foundation of discipling never occurs. Too many want world evangelization without paying the price of discipling a few people in order to get there.

The most important concern of an evangelist must be to lay a foundation of building a few disciples at the beginning of His ministry in order that effective outreach to the masses may take place in the future. The only way this will take place is by concentrating upon a few people. "A few people so dedicated in time will shake the world for God. Victory is never won by the multitudes."[6]

Many evangelists spread themselves thin and try to reach everybody in their congregation and their community. The result of their efforts is that instead of reaching everyone, they reach no one. Their efforts would have been far more effective if they had just reached a few.

Walter Henrichsen illustrates this point by telling of a deer hunt where the main objective was to kill as many deer as possible. During the hunt, he finds thirty or forty deer grazing at a clearing. Upon seeing the deer, he has to make a choice which gun he will use to shoot the deer. He has with him two guns, a 30.06 rifle and a 20-gauge shotgun. Which one should he use? If he uses the shotgun, he could hit almost every deer. If he used the rifle, he would only hit one or two. Many people would argue to use the shotgun in order to hit them all instead of using the rifle and hitting just a few. But the problem is that if one uses the shotgun, all the deer will be hit but none will be killed. If the rifle is used, most of the deer will be missed, but there will be one or two that can be taken home.[7]

This illustration easily applies to the outreach of the church. Many methods are like using a shotgun. Many people are hit by the approach but there are no people to take home. Churches today need rifle approaches where some may be missed, but at least a few will be hit to such an extent that they will be going to that heavenly home. It does no good to touch everybody if everyone is touched only to an extent that they all are able to leave like the deer hit by the shotgun. Only when some are hit to the extent that they stay and become disciples are churches fulfilling Christ's plan.

# IT IS FINISHED

If Jesus had only touched the multitudes, His ministry would not have had the impact that it did on the world. His ministry was powerful because He trained a few. After Christ had ascended and the Holy Spirit had come on the day of Pentecost, the plan was dependent upon the disciples — Jesus was counting on them. It was now a matter of whether or not those few to whom Jesus 'had devoted His life were really trained. What happens within the next thirty years of church growth tells us that they were.

Jesus completed His job of training His disciples, and He did it well. His statement in His prayer could be applied to the training that took place. "I have brought you glory on earth by completing the work you gave me to do" (John 17:4, NIV). On the cross, in speaking of His redemptive work, Jesus said, "It is finished" (John 19:30). In this passage Jesus had finished the great plan of redemption, but in the prayer in John 17, the work that He had finished is something different. In the context of this prayer, the work he had finished was the training of His men. He gave His life on the cross for millions for all time, but in that short three and a half year ministry, He gave His life to train twelve men.

## QUESTIONS

1. What are first, second, and third generation disciples?
2. What does Paul mean by the following phrases in 2 Timothy 2:2 — "the things you heard me say," "entrust," "reliable men," "who will teach others"?
3. How did Jesus initiate a plan for multiplication?
4. What are some other biblical examples of multiplying disciples?
5. Is the concentration of your ministry and that of your congregation more like that of a shotgun or a rifle? Explain.

6. What is the best way to lay a foundation at the beginning of a ministry?

7. At the end of His earthly ministry, what two things had He finished?

## FOOTNOTES

[1] Leroy Eims, *The Lost Art of Disciple Making* (Grand Rapids: Zondervan, 1978), p. 22.

[2] Allen Hadidian, *Successful Discipling* (Chicago: Moody Press, 1979), p. 38.

[3] Walter A. Henrichsen, *Disciples Are Made—Not Born* (Wheaton: Victor, 1974), p. 10.

[4] Robert Coleman, *The Master Plan of Evangelism* (Old Tappan: Fleming H. Revell, 1963), p. 21.

[5] William Barclay, *The Letters to the Galatians and Ephesians* (Philadelphia: Westminister, 1956), p. 104

[6] Coleman, p. 34.

[7] Henrichsen, p. 70-71.

# THE FOUR-PHASE FOLLOWING 6

S ince disciples are to be "conformed to the image of Christ" (Romans 8:29), it is important to examine where and how Jesus began to select His men. Upon examination, it appears that there were four phases in the development of the selection of His twelve. Therefore, it is important to identify these phases and see if they can correlate to similar phases for a discipler today.

## THE WAITING

The first phase in the selection of His disciples is marked by those who were waiting to believe.[1] After He had been baptized by John, Jesus began His public ministry in Galilee. As He went about the region teaching and performing miracles, a following started to occur. In this following, there were some people who were waiting to believe in Jesus. These were people who were ready to believe in Jesus. These were people who were ready to give their life to something; they simply did not know what.

Men who were among the first phase of the following were people like Andrew, Peter, Philip, Nathanael, and John. Two of them had already been followers of John the Baptist (John 1:35), and they were ready for the Lord for whom John had been making the way straight. These men were open and receptive to the message of Jesus. Some of them had already become intrigued with the message because of John's preaching. They were ready to "come and see" (John 1:46).

## THE EXAMINATION

The second phase in the following of Jesus is represented when these men began to examine Him. They took note of the words of John when he said, "Behold, the Lamb of God who takes away the sin of the world!" (John 1:29). During this phase, the would-be disciples became occasional companions of Jesus at convenient and usually festive times. The first four chapters of the gospel of John relate how they first began examining Jesus and became acquainted with Him at a marriage in Cana (John 2:1), at a passover in Jerusalem (John 2:13, 17, 22), on a visit to the place of John the Baptist's ministry (John 3:22), and on the return journey through Samaria from the south to Galilee (John 4:1-27, 31, 43-45).[2] During this second phase, based on their examination, these men began believing in Jesus, but their commitment to Him was not yet total.

## THE FOLLOWING

In the third phase, the level of involvement of these men increases. They now have become more than just occasional companions of the Messiah. Their fellowship is an uninterrupted attendance on His person which involves an entire or at least habitual abandonment of their secular occupations.[3] In this phase they were able to be exposed to various ministry situations. They were observers of how He cared for people and glorified God, they saw Him perform miracles and they heard His teaching. It is observable in the gospels how Peter, James, and John passed through these phases. They were ready and waiting having already been primed by John the Baptist. After His baptism, they began to examine Him, becoming occasional companions. As they began to follow Him, they started believing in Him to the point that they were willing to follow Him, completely forsaking their old way of life. It is seen, then, in the first three phases how these men are waiting to believe; they examine Jesus and then make a decision about Him based on their confrontation.

## THE CALL

The last phase of the following involved a new level of commitment. The fourth phase is where twelve were chosen by Jesus from His many followers and were formed into a select company to be trained for apostleship.

"And when day came, He called His disciples to Him; and chose twelve of them, whom He also named as apostles; Simon, whom He also named Peter, and Andrew his brother; James the son of Alphaeus, and Simon who was called the Zealot; Judas the son of James, and Judas Iscariot, who became a traitor" (Luke 6:13-16).

These twelve were to be specially trained by the Master and would be His witnesses in the world after He left. It would be up to them to give the world an accurate picture of Jesus' life and teachings.

As has been emphasized in earlier chapters, it is crucial for Christians today to pattern their lives and ministries after Jesus. It is only when Christians are following the plan of Jesus that they will have success. If Jesus had a four-phase following in His ministry, then it would be probable that there could be a four-phase following in the lives of disciples today. It is in a complete involvement of the four-phase following and the six levels of relationship (Chapter Seven) that disciples today can examine themselves and their ministry to see how close their pattern of discipling is to that of Jesus. The four phases of a disciple's following can be summarized by the pool of humanity, evangelistic activities, Bible study, and training.[5]

## THE POOL OF HUMANITY

If disciples are to be "fishers of men," then there needs to be a pond in which to do the fishing. In the case of Jesus, there were people around Him who were waiting to believe. In Jesus' case, there were people in all of life's situations who were there ready to hear His message. Some of them believed in Him, and others did not. The same situation exists today. There are people all around this world who have not put on Jesus as their Lord and Savior. Some of these people have been casually exposed to Jesus, others have not. Some of this group have been to church, others have not. Phase one includes those people who are waiting whom the Christians have not yet met, but they also include that pool of people with whom the Christian naturally comes in contact — friends, relatives, associates, and neighbors.

## EVANGELISTIC ACTIVITIES

The second phase of Jesus' following is where people started examining the man and His message. The church needs to provide activities and programs which will present the gospel and allow the people from phase one an opportunity to examine and make up their minds about Jesus. This might occur through evangelistic group Bible studies in neighborhoods where people are invited to come and informally study the Bible. Sunday school classes also provide an excellent opportunity to bring visitors who need to meet Jesus. A devotional or even a Sunday worship assembly can be an excellent place to bring someone in order for them to be exposed to the Lord and His people. If a church wants to be making disciples, it is important for that church to be bringing many visitors to many evangelistic activities.

Invitations and instruction can also be given through radio, T.V, newspapers and direct mail coverage to every home in the community.

It is also necessary to see this on an individual level. All church members ought to be constantly involving their friends, relatives, associates, and neighbors in all of the various evangelistic activities of the church. One who is truly striving to be a disciple will do his best to never come alone to these activities — he will bring someone. Evangelistic activities cannot be evangelistic if there are no non-Christians at them.

## THE BIBLE STUDY

After attending an evangelistic activity, some visitors will want to know more, or they will want to know how they can be partakers of the wonderful promises made by Jesus. Most evangelistic activities merely whet the people's appetites for more. Most people are converted to Jesus after they have personally been confronted in a one-on-one Bible study. As a result, Christians must be reaching out to the visitors of their evangelistic activities and making sure that they know how to become Christians. These individuals must be personally confronted about their sin and their need for a Savior. They should be confronted from God's Word with the power of the gospel and the hope of the new birth in Christ. It is here in the third phase that one makes the decision to become a Christian and is baptized.

## TRAINING

After someone becomes a Christian, the church's responsibility is not over to that person. When someone is born physically, he is a baby. Likewise when someone is born again, he is a baby in Christ who needs help in order to grow to maturity. As Jesus trained the seventy, the twelve, and those closest to Him; so also disciples today must be training new Christians. In this fourth phase, edifying and equipping (as mentioned in Chapter Three) takes place. The training phase is "for the equipping of the saints for the work of service, to the building up of the body of Christ" (Ephesians 4:12). This is the phase that some churches might call "follow-up." Is is in this phase that 2 Timothy 2:2 is best applied.

The four phases of Jesus and a disciple are illustrated in Table #2.

---

### Table #2
### The Four Phase Following of Jesus

| Jesus | Phases | Disciples Today |
|---|---|---|
| The Waiting | 1 | Pool of Humanity |
| The Examination | 2 | Evangelistic Activities |
| The Following | 3 | Bible Study |
| The Call | 4 | Training |

---

It becomes apparent how a person might go through all four phases. For example, John Nonmember works as a salesman at a department store. John has gone to church only as a child. He has a nominal, intellectual belief in God and has recently become interested in religion after watching a religious television program. One day, Joe Churchmember is shopping in John's store, and John waits on Joe. Not only does Joe buy a shirt from John, but he also invites him to come over to his house Tuesday evening for a group Bible study. John agrees to come, and he does. John enjoys the group Bible study and continues to come to it for several weeks. Seeing his interest, Joe begins to study one-on-one with John. After several personal studies, John decides to turn his life over to Jesus and become a Christian. However, John and Joe's relationship does not end there. They continue to meet together weekly for prayer and Bible study, and they also go to church together. One week, John brought a friend to the group Bible study, and later both John and Joe studied together with John's friend. Joe continued to spend time with John to help him mature in the Lord.

In this example, John goes through all four phases mentioned in this chapter. When he was at the store in the beginning, he was a part of the pool of humanity, phase one. When he started attending the group Bible study, he entered into phase two, the evangelistic activity. The third phase took place when John and Joe studied the Bible together and John became a Christian. The training stage, phase four, took place when Joe studied with John after his conversion, helped him grow in his church life, accompanied him in trying to win someone else to Christ, and generally associated with him.

Not only can Jesus be seen in the first four phases attributed to Him, but His life also is seen closely in the second four phases. In Jesus' ministry, He was continually associating Himself with the pool of humanity. He devoted Himself to a few but He never neglected the masses. He was always involved enough in the multitudes to be there to touch someone who was waiting to believe. Jesus did not limit his ministry to the temple or synagogue but was also in the marketplace where people were who needed to encounter Him. Jesus was also involving these people in evangelistic activities. It might be said that there were evangelistic activities wherever Jesus was. Often when He was among the crowds, He would speak to them and teach them. Other times, he would perform miracles. These acts, obviously, moved people to examine Him more closely. But Jesus did not leave His confrontations long distance. He also confronted individuals with their true needs as is evidenced by Jesus' encounter with Nicodemus, the woman at the well, Zaccheus, and many more. On top of all this, Jesus continually had with Him those people whom He was discipling. They were with Him sometimes exclusively in phase four, but often times they were with Him as He encountered people in other phases. A remarkable aspect of Jesus' ministry is that He did not neglect any phase but consistently touched people in all four phases.

If disciples today are to pattern their ministries after Jesus, they also must not neglect any phase of the four phase following and continually seek to serve people in all four phases. It would be easy for a Christian to concentrate only in one area. One might be bringing people to activities but never personally confronting them with Jesus. Another might be leading many people to Jesus but never following up on any of them. Someone else might spend all of his time with Christians and not effectively reach people in the pool of humanity.

The most effective disciple will pattern his ministry after that of Jesus and try to have a balance in his life in all four phases. He will always try to spend some time where the people are waiting to believe and will try to make the most of this time. A disciple of Christ will not isolate himself and only associate with believers, because there are many people who have not heard and are open to Jesus. But they will only come to the Lord when one of His people goes to them. As a result, a disciple is in the marketplace. He is where people live and work. He is constantly bearing witness to those of the world that there is a better way. He and his congregation will attempt to reach people in whatever ways they can. They will take advantage of the mail, the press, and the electronic media; but these will only add to the outreach and never be intended to take away from the personal contact in the marketplace.

A disciple following in Jesus' manner will always be striving to bring some of the people he meets in the pool of humanity with him to various evangelistic activities.

He will bring visitors to worship and Sunday school. He will also bring people to evangelistic group Bible studies and whatever other activities the church sponsors. If there is a social activity at the church, he again will use this as an opportunity to introduce people to believers in Christ.

Not only will a disciple bring people to activities, but he will also see to it that his visitor meets the person behind all of the activity — Jesus. He will see to it that there are always people in his life with whom he is trying to convert to Jesus. He will also make sure that these people have access to a Bible and possibly some good Christian literature. He will encourage them to examine first hand the good news of Jesus (cf. Colossians 4:16). There will always be a non-believer for whom he is praying and with whom he is studying. He will never let merely being with people or bringing someone to an activity suffice for actually bringing a soul to the Lord.

Conversions are not where the disciple stops. He continues to help new Christians mature in the Lord. Examining himself, he is always cognizant of equipping and discipling a few people who in turn will reproduce and participate also in all four phases of the four phase following.

## Questions

1. What are the four phases in Jesus' ministry? Explain these.
2. What are the four phases in a disciple's following today? Explain these.
3. In which of these four phases does your congregation have the greatest focus? The least?
4. In which of these four phases do you have the greatest focus? The least?
5. What do you need to do to have a balance in all four phases? What can your congregation do?

# FOOTNOTES

[1] Doug Hartman and Doug Sutherland, *A Guidebook to Discipleship* (Irvine: Harvest House, 1976), p. 47.

[2] Alexander Balmain Bruce, *The Training of the Twelve* (New Canaan: Keats, n.d.), p. 11.

[3] Bruce, p. 11.

[4] Bruce, p. 12.

[5] Hartman and Sutherland, p. 55.

# LEVELS
# OF
# RELATIONSHIP

**7**

**P** robably every minister has felt a great frustration because he was not able to minister to all the needs of all the people in his congregation. With all the demands that are made on him, a minister today cannot do all that he would like to do. If he is at a very large congregation, then he probably does not even know the names of all the members who attend. But even though it seems impossible, most ministers try to serve everyone's needs or at least touch everyone's life a little bit. The frustrating factor is that the more people with whom he spends his time the less effective he is with each one.

A minister asked his elders to write down on paper everything that they expected him to do during a week. After all the jobs were examined and time devoted to each one of them, this minister would have had to work 180 hours a week to do everything that was expected of him. Obviously, this had to be frustrating because once again, it seemed that the minister could not get his job done.

Being a full-time minister can often be frustrating because one so frequently fails to live up to his own expectations and also to those of others in the congregation. It is a realization of relief when one finally discovers that he cannot do more than Jesus did. Most ministers want to disciple everyone in their congregation at one time and forget that not even Jesus was able to disciple that many people. Ministers will only have peace when they stop trying to do more than Jesus. If Jesus was limited in the number of people whom He could disciple, everyone else will also be. Once a person realizes that he cannot personally do more than Jesus did in discipleship, then he can narrow down the field and get a proper start.

## JESUS' LEVELS OF RELATIONSHIP

With a careful examination of the life of Christ, it is noticeable that not all of Jesus' relationships were of the same intimacy. All of His relationships with people were good, but some of the relationships were closer than others. If disciples are to follow in the example of Jesus, it is important to analyze His levels of relationships and imitate them.

Gary Collins uses Illustration #8 as an example to show degrees of closeness in the life of Jesus.[1]

### Levels of Relationship

Dr. Collins illustrates the various degrees of closeness and how they relate to counseling, but this illustration can also teach some great truths about discipleship if its application is taken a few steps further.

Jesus is represented by the innermost circle and each concentric circle represents a level of relationship to Him with the lowest number representing the closest relationship. In terms of discipleship, it would seem that the apostle John occupied that level one relationship. John was seemingly the closest brother and friend to Jesus. John is referred to as the disciple whom Jesus loved several times (John 13:23; 19:26; 21:7; 21:20). Jesus loved all of his disciples but there seems to be a special love and intimacy between Jesus and John. As a result of this special relationship, John gives that unique pic-

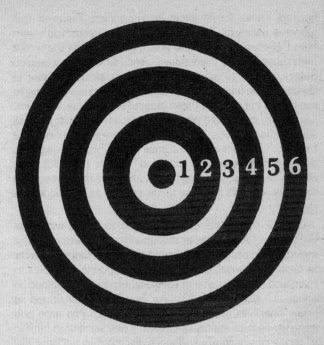

**Illustration 8**
**Levels of Relationship**

ture of Christ found only in his gospel.

John was also a part of Jesus' level two relationship which consisted of Peter, James, and John. These three seem to be closer to Jesus than any other people during His ministry. They accompanied Jesus with the other disciples, but on some occasions, they were chosen to be with Jesus when others were not. When Jesus healed Jairus' daughter, it was those three who were there. "And He allowed no one to follow Him, except Peter and James and John the brother of James" (Mark 5:37). When Jesus went upon the mountain and was transfigured, these three again accompanied Jesus at this glorious moment. "And six days later, Jesus took with Him Peter and James and John, and brought them to a high mountain by themselves. And He was transfigured before them" (Mark 9:2). In that most trying time in Gethsemane when Jesus was facing the crisis of going to the cross, He wanted these closest three to be with Him. "And they came to a place named Gethsemane; and He said to His disciples, 'Sit here until I have prayed.' And He took with Him Peter and James and John, and began to be very distressed and troubled" (Mark 14:32-33). The results of Jesus spending time with those three is seen in the book of Acts as these three emerge as the leaders of the early church.

On the third level of relationship to Jesus would be the twelve. "And it was at this time that He went off to the mountain to pray, and He spent the whole night in prayer to God. And when day came, He called His disciples to Him; and chose twelve of them, whom He also named as apostles" (Luke 6:12-13). As has been mentioned in other chapters, Jesus especially devoted His time and ministry to training these twelve. They were with Him in all types of situations and were discipled to become like Him.

On the fourth level in relationship to Jesus would be the seventy that Jesus appointed. "Now after this the Lord appointed seventy others, and sent them two and two ahead of Him to every city and place where He Himself was going to come" (Luke 10:1). The seventy were sent out and reported back to Jesus in similar fashion to that of the twelve. These seventy received special training from Jesus; however, their training was not as intensive as that of the twelve.

It becomes more difficult to identify levels of relationship past the fourth level. Perhaps on the fifth level could be the five hundred to whom he appears after His resurrection. This group is linked with some of the others who are close to Him. "He appeared to Cephas, then to the twelve, after that He appeared to more than five hundred brethren at one time . . . then He appeared to James, then to all the apostles" (1 Corinthians 15:5-7). Even if these were not the next closest group to Jesus, they obviously did not have as close a relationship as the seventy but had a relationship with Jesus that others did not have.

On the sixth level of relationship might be the crowds, the multitudes, or some of the larger groups of disciples that followed Jesus. When Jesus taught the sermon on the mount, it was not only to His lower levels of relationship but also to the multitudes (Matthew 5:1). In John 6 alongside the twelve, there were many other disciples. These disciples followed Jesus until the cost was too great for them (John 6:66-67).

The point of establishing these various relationships is to show that Jesus was closer to some people than He was to others. Some of His relationships were more intimate than others. However, to assume that Jesus' relationships on the outer levels were not good relationships would be making a wrong assumption. All of Jesus' relationships were good (at least on His part). Jesus had various levels of relationships, but on all levels the relationships were good. The difference in a number one relationship and a number five relationship was not that one was good and the other was bad but that one was more intimate than the other. Jesus was simply closer to someone on a level one than he would be to someone on a level five. But Jesus had as good a relationship as was possible to have on a level five with those on that level.

When Jesus became human, he was forced to live within the boundaries of space and time. Since He was bound within space and time as other humans are, there were a limited amount of relationships which He had, and there was a limited amount of time which He could spend with certain individuals. As a result, Jesus could not spend His time with everyone, or especially train everyone.

On the other hand, it was important that everyone with whom Jesus came into contact had a good encounter. Jesus demonstrated the same love to someone on a higher level as He did to those closest to Him. The difference is that some were able to receive a greater quantity of His love, but they did not receive a greater quality. Jesus loved the woman with a hemorrhage in Mark 5 just as much as He loved Peter, but she did not have the same level of relationship with Jesus that Peter had. Peter was on level two, she might have been on six. Why could Jesus not have a level one relationship with everyone? He could not because He was fully human and bound by space and time. He also could not because He was committed to a ministry of discipleship which focuses on a few.

It is also important to note that Jesus not only had good relationships at all levels but He also had relationships at all levels. Jesus did not forsake the crowds to only be with a few. He was with the crowds and concentrated on a few. He did not neglect the masses but made the most of the little time He would have with them. But Jesus did not limit himself to teaching the masses because He knew that a greater amount of time must be devoted to the few if they were to be trained.

## QUESTIONS

1. What kinds of problems do you face because there are so many people, not only in the world but also in your congregation?

2. Why can't we be close to everyone in our congregation and disciple many people? Why couldn't Jesus?

3. Who composed Jesus' six levels of relationship?

4. Jesus not only had relationships at all levels but also good ones at all levels. How was this possible?

# FOOTNOTES

[1] Gary Collins, *How to Be a People Helper* (Santa Ana: Vision House, 1976), p. 38.

# APPLYING THE LEVELS

8

## LEVELS IN TODAY'S CHURCH

If disciples are to be like Jesus, then they need to imitate His levels of relationship. Some Christians feel guilty when they have close brothers or sisters in the Lord. They feel guilty because they are closer to some Christians than they are to others. Disciples today must come to the realization that they are bound by the same factors that bound Jesus — space and time. No one can have an intimate spiritual relationship with everyone. Close levels of relationships are limited to only a few people. This was a limitation in Jesus' ministry and it will be for every human being.

As a result, disciples today must imitate Jesus' example in His relationships. The two factors that must be applied are (1) disciples should have relationships at all six levels and (2) all the levels should be good relationships.

Disciples today must examine their lives to see if there are indeed people who are currently on all six levels. It is easy to have relationships on some levels but not on all of them. To be like Jesus, the disciple must be filling his life with all levels of relationship.

How would this apply to a Christian brother who was interested in making and multiplying disciples? On level one, he would need to have a closest brother with whom he could share. These two would be best of friends and there would be a great depth to their spiritual intimacy. They would pray together and share in their insights of God's Word. For such a close relationship to exist, there would need to be a vulnerability on both of their parts in order for them to be into each other's lives. No brother would be a greater encouragement than this brother, and he would be open to his rebukes because he is convicted of the genuineness of his love. These two would spend much time together in many and varied situations. They would become like-minded to each other and like-minded to Jesus.

On level two he would have a few brothers who would be close to Him. They would only be three or four in number. These brothers might be called a discipler group.[1] They would have a very close relationship similar to level one, but the perspective of the group would be broader because of the diversities and insights of a few more people. This group would also spend a lot of time together in all types of situations. They would grow together in a similar fashion to that on level one.

On level three would be a larger group, yet it would still be small. Jesus' level three had twelve. Some place near twelve would thus be a good size. This group would probably be a group that met together regularly for Bible study and prayer. They might be a group who work together in an evangelistic group Bible study. In an evangelistic study, they would not only be studying together but also working together to bring people to Christ (an important factor in all of the first three levels).

Level four would be an even larger group. This would probably be a Sunday school class that meets regularly for Bible studies and has other activities which the members do together periodically. This level four is assuming that the Sunday school class is larger than a small group as in level three.

Level five would in this illustration probably consist of his local congregation, and level six might be his town or a section of his city. It could even be a place of employment or a school if he were a student.

The levels of relationships might vary according to the size of the particular congregation. The previous example would be possible levels of relationship for the Northwest Church of Christ in Seattle, Washington. This congregation has been discipling many students from the University of Washington. Many of these students have relationships at all levels. On level one, they have a prayer covenant; on level two they have a discipler group; on level three they have an evangelistic group Bible study; on level four, they are a part of the campus ministry which has devotionals and Bible classes; on level five they are members of the Northwest Church of Christ; and on level six, they have their community at the University of Washington.

Again, the point of the concept is that the disciple who is conforming to Jesus will try to have relationships on all six levels and also have good relationships on all six levels. A good understanding of this concept will help end the frustration that many have who have realized that they cannot know or minister to everyone. The key then becomes to make sure one has some good close relationships, and then instead of feeling guilty about the distant ones, the most should be made of them with what little time exists. If a disciple, who has relationships on all levels, only spends about five minutes a week with another brother who is on level five, he should not be discouraged that he only has five minutes but should make that five minutes the best possible, thus establishing a good level five. A problem would only occur if this five minutes were not quality time or if one of these brothers did not have any relationships at lower levels.

# DISCIPLING IN THE LEVELS

Since the focus of this research is in discipleship, it is important to understand how the levels of relationships relate to multiplying disciples. It has been stated that a disciple imitates Jesus, and Jesus had good relationships on all six levels. Therefore a disciple should also have good relationships on all six levels. But discipleship as has been studied in this research actually only takes place on levels one, two, and three. The reason that discipling can only take place on the first three levels was established in earlier chapters by the fact that effective discipling can only take place with a few people. Since levels four through six involve relationships with large groups of people, true discipleship does not take place.

When this observation is studied in context of churches today, a big problem emerges. If discipleship takes place on levels one, two, and three and the church is to be making disciples, then there should be a great focus in the church on establishing good levels of relationship on the first three levels. But the problem is that most churches concentrate on the fifth level predominately and secondarily on the fourth.

The major focus of most churches is on their fifth level which would be their congregational assembly. Most of the leadership spends the majority of their time and preparation for the Sunday assembly. This fifth level usually takes a higher priority than the other levels. In fact, it is often done at the exclusion of other levels of relationships. As a result, when there is not a focus on the first three levels, discipling does not occur.

Probably the second focus of churches would be on the educational program or Sunday school. Although this is very important, it is still only level four, and discipleship does not occur until level three. Some churches have their entire ministries centered around only worship assembly and Sunday school. If a congregation supposes that a person who only attends Sunday school and assembly will become a multiplying disciple, it is quite mistaken because that person is missing out on the very levels that provide true discipleship.

When this is further analyzed, it becomes apparent why some individuals never reach maturity, or congregations for that matter. If a Christian only has a level four and five relationship, he will never mature to the point of being a multiplying disciple. Yet a person who regularly attends Sunday school and assembly is viewed by many as being mature. In many congregations, members neglect Bible school and merely come to the assembly. In this case, the member only has a level five relationship, and this has nothing to do with whether this level five relationship is even a good one. Incidentally, it is very difficult to have good level fives if there are not any relationships more intimate because the person tends to feel like merely a stranger in the crowd.

With this same reasoning, it is easy to see that many congregations are not mature and producing many disciples. When there are not many members in a church who have good relationships at all levels, then it means that there are not many members who are being discipled. Without discipleship, the hope for an extended church growth and maturity will be nil.

After an observation of the maturing of new Christians at the Northwest Church of Christ in Seattle, several important factors have been noticed. Some of the new Christians in this congregation have reached a maturity in Christ very quickly as opposed to others who seem to be struggling along with the elementary principles. It has been noticed in reflection that the ones who matured quickly were the ones who had good relationships at many levels. Many of the conversions at this congregation are college students who have come through evangelistic Bible studies (level three). Upon their conversion they were encouraged to have a brother or sister to study with, pray with, and disciple them (level one). These new Christians also became a part of the Bible studies and devotionals of the campus ministry (level four). They also became active members of the Northwest congregation (level five). Some of these became a part of the discipler groups (level two). It was noted that these new Christians matured very quickly and also reproduced themselves in others.

When these new Christians are compared with others who were converted in other ways, something striking is noticed. Others who became Christians simply were baptized after only attending assembly or Sunday school and assembly. Some of these new Christians never developed any other levels of relationship after their baptism than these two (levels four and five). The observation is that these new Christians have not matured or reproduced like the other new Christians. The difference is that some were discipled and some were not.

A new Christian who has good relationships on all levels will achieve a maturity in Christ that is greater than other Christians who have been Christians for years but only have relationships on levels four and five. A new Christian with good relationships at all levels could, within a year, have a deeper grasp of Christianity and a stronger faith than an older Christian of thirty years who only had levels four and five. This helps one to realize the why of what has been known all along — that maturity is not dependent upon how long one has been a Christian.

## LEVELS FOR LEADERS

This information concerning levels of relationship is very important for church leaders. Leaders of churches must be examples in developing good relationships in all areas. Because of pressures, it is easy to only focus in levels four and five because this is where most of the people are. There is also pressure to focus on these two levels because that is the expectation of most and it is immediately the most visible. Some church leaders have not extended themselves into the lower levels because of the myth that ministers should not have close relationships with the members.

However, if the church leaders are not examples in developing relationships on the first three levels, discipleship will have to come from other parts of the congregation. Some leaders are not attracted to the first three levels because they are not as noticeable and also because they are concerned with the masses.

Many leaders are not patient enough to work with the few to achieve the greater growth. But a congregation will be limited in its scope if its leaders are not having good relationships on levels one through three. This is because they will have leaders who are not making disciples.

A leader must realize that he cannot have relationships on the first three levels with many. This may be frustrating, but it must always be remembered that a discipling ministry starts small and multiplies. At any given time, a leader can only have a few good intimate relationships. However, his goal for the congregation is that everyone would have good relationships with people at all levels. Although he would not have relationships with many on the lower levels, he would want everyone in his congregation to have the lower levels of relationship with someone. The frustrating part of this is that it will not be this way overnight. As maturity does not come overnight for an individual, neither does it for a church. However, an examination of the amount of people who have good relationships on all levels will give a leader a tool for measuring maturity.

From this study it becomes apparent that, since discipleship does not occur until people relate in lower levels, leaders need to not only develop these lower levels of relationship in their personal lives, but also encourage them in their congregation.

## CONFLICTS IN CLIQUES

An objection to developing small groups and close relationships is that these form cliques or exclusive groups. This charge cannot be justified unless one is also prepared to claim that Jesus instigated cliques with His twelve.

Small groups and close relationships (levels one, two, and three) can be cliques but they do not have to be. Cliques only form when there are bad relationships on some level. Remember, the goal is not only to have relationships on all levels but also good ones on all levels. A clique would result when one concentrated on the lower levels without having good relationships on the upper levels. A clique results when the people in the lower levels devote themselves to each other to such an extent that they neglect people in levels four, five, and six. Because these people have been neglected on their level, they become jealous or resentful of the exclusion from the inner circles and claim that a clique has been formed.

It is true that someone on an outer level might be jealous that he is not on an inner level even though an attempt has been made to have a good relationship with him. If this occurs, the entire process of discipling should be explained to him telling him how there is a limited number of people any one person can disciple. Ultimately, selection must take place if discipleship is to occur, and some may respond improperly if they are not chosen. However, if some are not excluded and others selected to spend time with on the lower levels, relationships will never occur which will cause disciples to multiply. The concept of selection will be covered in Chapter Twelve. The best a disciple can do is to have good relationships in all levels. This is what Jesus did — we can do no more.

# CHRISTIANITY IS RELATIONAL

Discipleship is a part of Christianity, and Christianity is relational. Christians not only have a vertical relationship with God to whom they have been reconciled, but they also have horizontal relationships with each other. It is important, therefore, to note in this place that true discipleship cannot take place outside the body of Christ, the church. To do this would be saying that all that is needed for a disciple is a vertical relationship or lower level relationships.

The church is necessary and important for a disciple. Otherwise, God would not have made the church. God's plan could have been for disciples to each simply have individual relationships with Him, but He didn't. Instead He wanted disciples to not only have a personal relationship with Him but also a corporate relationship with the body of Christ.

Too many people that have made decisions for Jesus have not been incorporated into the body of Christ. In the early church when someone was baptized into Christ that also meant that they were a part of the body (1 Corinthians 12:13) and the Lord added them to the church (Acts 2:47). The need for the church is just as crucial today as it was then.

Many people could be reached through campaigns, religious organizations or traveling evangelists. But if these are not a part of the church, they will never be disciples. New Christians need something that is lasting. Too many have been reached by a group on campus or an evangelistic crusade who have never been seen at a church assembly or had anything to do with the Lord since. If all of these had truly been genuine conversions and they had all been discipled, the world could have been taken for Christ by this present time. But religious organizations and evangelists come and go. And when all of these have come and gone, the church will still stand. Therefore, if disciples are ever to be discipled they must relate to the church.

The mark of a disciple, "to love one another," that was discussed previously can best be seen by the world as it looks at the church. If a disciple does not love the church, then he does not have good relationships on all levels.

Really the whole problem of giving personal care to every believer is only resolved in a thorough understanding of the nature and mission of the church. It is well here to observe that the emergence of the church principle around Jesus, whereby one believer was brought into fellowship with all others, was the practice in a larger dimension of the same thing that He was doing with the twelve. Actually it was the church that was the means of following up all those who followed Him. That is, the group of believers became the body of Christ, and as such ministered to each other individually and collectively.[2]

## QUESTIONS

1. What two factors do we need to imitate today in Jesus' example in relationships?

2. What could be examples of people who would compose the six levels of relationship in your life?

3. Are there any levels of relationship that you are missing in your life? What are they?

4. Are there any levels in which the relationships are not good? Which ones?

5. After analyzing Jesus' levels of relationship and that in most churches today, what are some apparent reasons for our lack of making disciples?

6. On which levels of relationship does your congregation focus?

7. Why do you think that there is a lack of example in leaders today in concentrating on the lower levels of relationship?

8. How can we develop close relationships and still avoid cliques?

9. Why is it so important for discipleship to take place in the church and not separate from it?

## FOOTNOTES

[1] Doug Hartman and Doug Sutherland, *A Guidebook to Discipleship* (Irvine: Harvest House, 1976), p. 97.

[2] Robert Coleman, *The Master Plan of Evangelism* (Old Tappan: Fleming H. Revell, 1963), p. 46.

# RELATIONAL AND TERMINAL THINKING

9

When someone is lost in a city, it would do little good to ask directions from a tourist. When someone is lost, he wants directions that will lead him to his destination. Tourists are full of activity and see many sights but never stay long enough in a place to know their way around. Many people in the church treat Christianity like tourists. They see and do many activities but never truly know where they are going.

From other chapters, it can be seen that the church needs to be convicted about making disciples. There are some who have this conviction in their head, but they have not borne the fruit of a disciple in their lives. One reason might be that they do not know where they are going. They are in the right place, but they are still wandering around like a tourist. The difference in a tourist and a disciple is that a disciple knows where he is going. The reason that one knows where he is going and the other does not, may have to do with their way of thinking. The tourist may be thinking in a wrong manner. A disciple's way of thinking is drastically changed from the way he thought before. Paul puts it this way: "And do not be conformed to this world, but be transformed by the renewing of your mind, that you may prove what the will of God is, that which is good and acceptable and perfect" (Romans 12:2). A disciple's mind has been renewed.

In Lewis Carroll's great story, *Alice's Adventures in Wonderland*, he tells of an interesting encounter between the heroine and the Cheshire Cat. After meeting this good natured feline, Alice inquired about the direction of her journey, and the cat's answer has great applications to a tremendous dilemma of our society and one of the major reasons for a lack of effectiveness in discipleship.

"Chesire Puss," she began, rather timidly, as she did not at all know whether it would like the name; however, it only grinned a little wider. "Come, it's pleased so far," thought Alice, and she went on. "Would you tell me, please, which way I ought to walk from here?" "That depends a good deal on where you want to get to," said the Cat. "I don't much care where —" said Alice. "Then it doesn't matter which way you walk," said the Cat. "So long as I get somewhere," Alice added as an explanation. "Oh you're sure to do that," said the Cat, "if you only walk long enough."[1]

One of the greatest problems of our society which filters into the church is that Christians are like Alice and do not know where they are going. Alice, just like people today, wanted directions. Society is crying out for help and asking for guidance, but the problem is that they do not know where they are going. As a result, society listens to whatever source of direction that is currently popular and is swayed to go down numerous dead end streets. They keep wandering aimlessly through life, bouncing back and forth like a pinball because they have not properly designated their destination. A roadmap does no good if one does not know where he is going. The Cheshire Cat knew that any road would serve Alice if she did not know where she wanted to be at the end of the road. When people do not know where they are going, this gives great opportunity for cults, hedonism and the other popular philosophies of the time.

A contemporary song by David Tao states the problem explicitly:

Where will you be when you get where you're going?
How will you know that you've taken the right way?
Nothing on earth can satisfy your deepest needs.
Who can be sure of anything today?[2]

The song expresses the mood of society — one of frustration and despair. With people moving but getting nowhere, one begins to doubt whether anything indeed can meet contemporary needs and lead to a place that is worthwhile. The song also speaks of what is probably the key problem of today's religion — not theology but epistemology. (Epistemology is the study of knowledge. It is concerned with the questions "How do you know?" and "How can I know?".) The songwriter cries out, "How can I know?" The question modern man must ask then is, "How do I know that I'm traveling on the right road?"

Since modern society does not know the end of its way, the means become confused. If one does not have an objective in life, it does not make any difference which means (or way of life) one chooses. It is not that the end justifies the means, but that there is no realized end; therefore, any means becomes acceptable.

As a result, modern man has no goals, or if he has goals, they are short term. The proverb which says "Aim at nothing and you will be sure to hit it" applies readily to today's society. If there is no desired end, then any means is bound to reach that end. In *The Master Plan of Evangelism*, Dr. Robert Coleman states in reference to Jesus:

"His life was ordered by His objective. Everything He did and said was a part of the whole pattern. It had significance because it contributed to the ultimate purpose of His life in redeeming the world for God. This was the motivating vision governing His behavior. His steps were ordered by it. Mark it well. Not for one moment did Jesus lose sight of His goal.[3]

Jesus' life ordered by objective is extremely different from today's haphazard lifestyles. Most people's lives are ordered by anything but objectives. Our educational philosophies and culture have taught us to think in a way other than by objectives. However, a disciple of Jesus Christ must learn to think in a manner that is drastically different from those of the world.

In their book, *A Guidebook to Discipleship,* Doug Hartman and Doug Sutherland describe two types of thinking — terminal and relational. " 'Relational' thinking is defined as the process of relating activities and knowledge to an objective. 'Terminal' thinking is defined as the process whereby activity and knowledge are objectives and ends within themselves."[4] It is important to understand these two types of thinking in order to understand "life by objective."

Terminal thinking begins early in a person's lifetime. If it has not begun by the time a child enters school, terminal thinking will begin there. Students are educated with terminal values. They know that to pass from one grade to the next they must learn X number of things and be able to communicate them by rote. The "why" for the knowledge is seldom learned. This education process often continues through his life and is even continued in the university. A business student memorizes a list of items that are either debits or credits, but too often fails to learn the significance of this to the entire function of accounting much less business in general. Through the educational system, students quickly learn that they do not have to understand the far-reaching purpose of a subject in order to receive a good grade. As a result, people are conditioned to think terminally and do not relate the activities of life to an ultimate objective.[5]

This manner of thinking is not only manifested in our educational process but is also mixed into other areas of life. If a person thinks terminally in small matters, he will reflect the same thought process in the more important matters of life. When it comes to answering those crucial questions of "What am I doing here?" and "What is my purpose?", modern man does not know how to find the answers. Since the answers are not readily available or even conceivably ascertainable, he will store the questions in the back of his head, and his life becomes directed by his activities.

The plight of most Americans is that they have not found answers to the fundamental questions of life and do not know where to look for answers. As a result, they fill their lives with activities and relationships. These do not relate to anything but merely occupy time and fill one's life with activity. Therefore, a person's activities rule the direction of his life. Activities are only seen in a terminal manner. One goes to work, plays racquetball, goes to a movie, takes the children to the zoo, but the reason behind these activities is neither seen nor questioned. They are merely activities which occupy time, and as long as time is filled, one does not have to think about fundamental questions of existence. One's existence finally becomes a number of unrelated activities and relationships that occupy one's time. The activities govern the person rather than the person or a value governing the activity. It becomes very difficult to find reasons for doing one thing as opposed to another if nothing relates to a purpose. As a result, society has adopted a philosophy of "if it feels good, do it."

This same terminal mind set not only applies in activities but also in relationships. If a person does not have a frame of reference, relationships are terminal also. Woody Allen expressed this well in the closing statement of his Oscar winning movie, *Annie Hall*. A man goes to the psychiatrist on behalf of a friend. He tells the doctor that his friend fancies himself as a chicken. "Why don't you bring him in for treatment?" the psychiatrist asked. The man responded, "Oh, I would; but we need the eggs."[6] In this statement Woody Allen takes an existential view of life and comments that the world in which he lives is utterly absurd. Although the world and the people in it do not relate, he still needs the relationships. There is neither reason behind the relationships nor a purpose to hold them together, but without them life is not as valuable. Allen rejects reason in the universe and to make his life meaningful, he fills it with relationships. The relationships occupy his time and fill up his life with activity so there is less time to focus on the meaning behind the relationships and the meaning behind life. Relationships thus become an aversion to seeking the purpose of life and are terminal. Although they do not relate, he still needs them like the eggs. Therefore, terminal thinking could not only be a lifestyle where activities govern one's life but also where unrelated relationships determine one's life.

It quickly becomes apparent that terminal thinking is not merely an educational process, a way of looking at activities, or a reason for personal relationships. It is more than all this — it is a way of life. Terminal thinking can even be a part of church-goers. Many people attend church and never stop to analyze why they are there. Maybe it has become habitual. But too many people are sitting in church pews without consciously relating why they are there to their ultimate purpose. As a result, it is even possible for church-goers to be terminal thinkers.

Relational thinking is the opposite of terminal thinking. A relational thinker relates everything he learns and everything he does to his objective in life. The apostle Paul made a statement of relational thinking when he said, "And whatsoever you do in word or deed, do all in the name of the Lord Jesus" (Colossians 3:17).

Doug Hartman and Doug Sutherland tell the story of a campus minister who inquired into the life of university students concerning relational thinking:

> He would ask questions such as "Why did you come here to this university?" The answers he would get were often times comical answers like, "I came to college because I didn't know what to do," or "My parents expect me to go to college and they are paying the bill." He would then ask, "But why do you go to class, what is your

objective?" The student would usually answer, "If you want to get good grades you gotta go to class." He would ask, "Is that your purpose for life — to get good grades?" The student would usually get kind of indignant at this point and respond, "Of course not, (pause) if you want to graduate you gotta get good grades." "Is that your purpose in life to graduate?" The student, now getting a little nervous, "You gotta graduate in order to get a good job, to give security to your wife, so you can have cute kids." "Is that your reason for existence, your ultimate purpose — to have cute kids?" The student — "Listen, I would like to talk some more, but I gotta go to class."[7]

This student is not alone in this type of reasoning. Many students do not have a purpose for their major. People take various types of jobs without ever examining how this job fits into their ultimate purpose for life. Does it matter what someone majors in, what kind of job a person has, or what kind of activity someone does? It only matters if one is a relational thinker.

One might question whether he can make an accounting job relate. It is possible to be merely an accountant, or one could be an accountant for Christ. What is the difference? The difference is seen in whether the accountant relates his job to his ultimate purpose. Before this can take place, a determination of one's ultimate purpose is necessary. The prophet Isaiah gives helpful insight into what a human being's ultimate purpose is: "Every one who is called by My name, and whom I have created for My glory, whom I have formed even whom I have made" (Isaiah 43:7). This passage makes it clear that people were created for the purpose of glorifying God. Therefore, if an accountant is a relational thinker, he is an accountant to glorify God. How can this take place? An accountant can do his work "as for the Lord." He can be an example of how a Christian is a hard worker and implement the lifestyle of Jesus at work. He can also see the people that are his customers and with whom he works as people who need Jesus. He can put in a good word for

Jesus when opportunities arise. A relational accountant would have the conviction that God put him in his particular environment to be a witness and thus glorify Him.

When a disciple truly becomes a relational thinker even those previously inconsequential times can become very important. A relational thinker can ride a bus or plane for Jesus by noticing the people around him and being a witness of God's grace.

A disciple who is relational will eat for Jesus. He begins to use those times when he is eating for more than filling his stomach. He will plan on eating with non-Christians to lead them to Christ, eating with Christians to enjoy fellowship, and even seeing waitresses not as people who serve but who need to be served. People who are family members are now more than family. They are people who need the Lord, and are some of the most likely people to be led to Christ. Activities also become relational. Instead of having a party, a relational person has a party for a purpose — either to introduce non-believers to Christians or to further develop a relationship with a Christian. Everything is done for the purpose of relating to his ultimate objective. Recreational events like racquetball now are more than just exercise. It is exercise to keep the body, the temple of God, in shape as a glory to God. A relational racquetball player might be concerned with whom he would be playing. He might play with someone who ordinarily would not come to church or a Bible study in order to establish a relationship for future spiritual confrontation. The relational disciple also learns to capture the formerly wasted time in a day and relates those moments to His objective. Those small intervals or between times can be used for Bible reading or Scripture memorization. Nothing in his life is exempt from his objective — all must relate.

Many people have difficulty relating their work to their objective. Stanley Shipp was talking with a young doctor at Barnes Hospital in St. Louis about his profession. The doctor was showing Stanley the pathology laboratory to demonstrate the advances which had been made in medical technology. He showed Stanley a machine that he called "the spaghetti machine" because of a series of fourteen tubes which were a part of the machine. He explained how this machine analyzed blood in fourteen different ways at once, recorded the analyses on a graph and computer, translated it into numbers, and recorded the results on the patient's chart. Stanley asked, "What's that for?" The doctor responded, "It's for blood analysis to see what's wrong with the blood." Stanley inquired, "What for?" "To see what's wrong with the person," he replied. Again Stanley asked, "What for?" "So we can extend the life of the person," he explained. "What for?" "So the body can be kept alive for possibly five years longer," the doctor said. And once again the resounding question, "What for?"

Stanley explained to the doctor that it did little good if a person only extended a physical life and never dealt with the inner being because they will die in five years and be lost. He explained that the medical field was important but should not be divorced from care for the soul.[8]

Jesus knew His objective. He made His purpose for coming to the earth perfectly clear: "For the Son of Man has come to seek and to save that which was lost" (Luke 19:10). His daily activities were not without direction. "The next day He purposed to go forth into Galilee, and He found Philip, and Jesus said to him, 'Follow Me' " (John 1:43). This passage shows that Jesus did not haphazardly go places but purposed to go to particular destinations for a reason. His activities did not govern His life, but His objective ruled His activities. Jesus' total relational lifestyle is best seen when He responded to the Pharisees and said, "I know where I came from and where I am going" (John 8:14). This passage demonstrates that Jesus not only knew how His past related but had also planned for the relationship of His future events. Jesus knew that He would die in Jerusalem, but in spite of this, "He resolutely set His face to go to Jerusalem" (Luke 9:51). Jesus knew how His death related to the redemption of mankind.

The apostle Paul also knew his objective. To the Corinthians, he declared, "Do you not know that those who run in a race all run, but only one receives the prize? Run in such a way that you may win" (1 Corinthians 9:24). Paul is, in his words, telling them how to be ordered by an objective or to be a relational thinker. He gives himself as an example of this — "Therefore I run in such a way, as not without aim; I box in such a way, as not beating the air; but I buffet my body and make it my slave, lest possibly, after I have preached to others, I myself should be disqualified" (1 Corinthians 9:26-27).

When a disciple learns to think relationally, the "concentration principle" comes into play. The concentration principle can be defined as "whatever captures a man's mind; captures him and becomes his true objective."[9] The Proverb writer puts it this way, "For as he thinks within himself, so he is" (Proverbs 23:7). As a result, when a disciple becomes a relational thinker and applies the concentration principle, his ultimate objective becomes a part of him. His new way of thinking where more things relate to his objective becomes habitual. Indeed his lifestyle is being transformed by the renewing of his mind (Romans 12:2).

A disciple with a renewed mind not only thinks in a relational manner but also in a manner that is on a higher plane than that of someone in the world. Paul expresses this to the Philippians, "Finally, brethren, whatever is true, whatever is honorable, whatever is right, whatever is pure, whatever is lovely, whatever is of good repute, if there is any excellence and if anything worthy of praise, let your mind dwell on these things" (Philippians 4:8). He again states this idea to the Colossians, "Set your mind on the things above, not on the things that are on earth" (Colossians 3:2).

God can use people of all walks of life. Many Christians think that only full-time ministers have dynamic ministries. But when relational thinking is properly understood, every disciple is a full time minister because everyone has a ministry and everything in one's life can relate to his ministry. When this concept is realized, it gives greater self-value to those disciples who are in secular jobs. God can use every Christian in a dynamic way. Many Christians have not realized this, and as a result, they do not regard the importance of their ministries very highly. When Christians learn to relate all of their lives to their ultimate purpose, then there will be happier churches because everyone will know that they are as important as any other member, and they can quit feeling guilty for activities that are not directly related to the church. Churches will also start growing faster when they have relational thinking members because these Christians will be people who are reaching out to people at work, in the neighborhoods and wherever they go.

In the New Testament, evangelism was the responsibility of everyone in the church, and it was relational. "Those who had been scattered preached the word wherever they went" (Acts 8:4, NIV). In this passage it is evident that the message of Christ was a part of their lives that accompanied them in all places. As the early Christians were scattered, the mission of the church was not hampered but helped. These early Christians did not see evangelism as what they did as much as it was what they were. When they were scattered, they probably did not have organized programs for converting people, but the message was a part of them and was shared in natural situations wherever they went, and the church grew. Similarly, the church will grow today at the same rate only when evangelism is not merely seen as a program but as a lifestyle. Every member of the church must see how his lifestyle relates to evangelism. When a church begins to practice lifestyle evangelism, it means that every church member is sharing the good news of Jesus in his or her everyday activities of life — mothers, fathers, businessmen, homemakers, teachers, clerks, doctors, lawyers, employees, and students.[10]

The results of lifestyle evangelism where every church member is relating his position in life as an opportunity for evangelism would be staggering. The Mormons have discovered that they make only 0.1% converts for every 1,000 doors knocked. They also found that when a Mormon uses his home as a place of evangelism that the success rate increases to 50%. They have learned that their most effective contacts are made by the rank and file members through business, family, and social ties.[11]

All kinds of evangelism are good and important, but the most lasting and far reaching is when everyone is relating his lifestyle to his purpose. The early Christians shared the gospel in all situations whether they were public or private. "Day after day, in the temple courts and from house to house, they never stopped teaching and proclaiming the good news that Jesus is the Christ" (Acts 5:42, NIV).

To become a relational thinker, there are basically three steps: (1) determining the ultimate purpose of life, (2) defining the activities of life in terms of the purpose, (3) evaluating the activities to see if they lead to the purpose.[12]

Obviously in becoming a relational thinker, one must first determine his ultimate purpose. Otherwise, he is doomed to be a terminal thinker. If the relational thinker is to be a disciple of Christ, then his ultimate purpose must be to glorify God (Isaiah 43:7). The way that one glorifies God is two-fold, but both aspects involve relationships. The first relationship in glorifying God that needs to be developed is the relationship with God. This is done through prayer and Bible study. The second relationship that needs to be developed is one's relationship with other people. This might be called a Christian's ministry. To glorify God, disciples not only develop a close relationship with God but also develop their ministries with people. These people would include Christians and non-Christians. It includes evangelism, service, benevolence, edification, and all other acts of true love. It is developing a ministry which deals with people in the manner of Jesus.

After one's ultimate purpose is determined and understood, a relational thinker begins to define all of his activities, words, and thoughts in his life in terms of his purpose. He begins to ask questions of his activities — "Does this relate?" "Is this glorifying?" "Would something else be more glorifying at this present time?" At first, this might seem to eliminate one's freedom in Christ, but when it is properly understood it helps one to realize freedom at the maximum. One might think that this analyzation of activities would eliminate all leisure or recreational activities. On the contrary, it would not eliminate them but give them purpose. Suppose a Christian is determining whether or not to play tennis. If he could relate this activity to glorifying God and believed that this was a proper time to do it, he would do it. He might see this activity as developing his relationship to God because through it he is keeping in shape his body which is the temple of God, and at this present time, he is needing some exercise to keep in shape. He might also see this act as something to develop his ministry. This action might further his relationship with a Christian or non-Christian. But if this activity could not be related at this present time, the relational thinker would not do it.

After one has determined his purpose and activities, he needs to continuously evaluate his activities in order to see if these activities did indeed relate. After living relationally and evaluating these activities consistently, one can learn not simply to choose good activities but the best.

## QUESTIONS

1. What are some examples of how today's society is aimlessly wandering without a sense of direction?

2. What is the difference between relational and terminal thinking?

3. How has terminal thinking been manifested in our society?

4. How can you relate your occupation to your purpose; or can you?

5. What are some biblical passages which demonstrate that Jesus and Paul were relational thinkers?

6. What is lifestyle evangelism? How could you have a more evangelistic lifestyle?

## FOOTNOTES

1 Lewis Carroll, *Alice in Wonderland* (New York: Peebles, n.d.), p. 71.

2 David Tao, "Where Will You Be When You Get Where You're Going?" *Rejoice and Sing to the Lord,* (Vol. II, eds. Reid Lancaster and Garly L. Mabry (Austin: Sweet, n.d.), p. 37.

3 Robert Coleman, *The Master Plan of Evangelism* (Old Tappan: Fleming H. Revell, 1963), p. 34.

4 Doug Hartman and Doug Sutherland, *A Guidebook to Discipleship* (Irvine: Harvest House, 1976), p. 31.

5 Hartman and Sutherland, p. 31.

6 Mike Reimer, "He Needs the Eggs," *His,* December, 1979, p.14.

7 Hartman and Sutherland, p. 33.

8 Sermon by Stanley Shipp ("What For?") White River Christian Camp, Crosbyton, Texas, (tape available at Church of Christ Student Center, Lubbock, Texas).

9 Hartman and Sutherland, p. 34.

10 Chuck Lucas, "Lifestyle Evangelism," *At the Crossroads,* 24:5:1, February 8, 1981.

11 Lucas, p. 1.

12 Hartman and Sutherland, pp. 37-38.

# THE COST OF DISCIPLESHIP

# 10

Although the way of making disciples is the plan of Jesus and is the only method that will win the world to Christ, not everyone is going to adopt a discipling ministry. In Jesus' day there was opposition to His plan, and there will be today. In Jesus' ministry, it was often the religious who protested the loudest against His teaching. Because of certain barriers that result, frequently it is the religious world today which has the most trouble swallowing the commitment to make disciples.

## THE COST IS HIGH

Following Jesus might have seemed easy at first as one saw the multitudes surrounding Him. But it did not take long before a would-be follower met with the cost of discipleship. Jesus was asking His followers to commit their lives to Him completely. He demanded an exclusive attachment to Him and Him alone. "No servant can serve two masters; for either he will hate the one, and love the other, or else he will hold to one, and despise the other. You cannot serve God and mammon" (Luke 16:13).

When one decided to follow in the way of Jesus, it meant that he was to forsake completely his old life of sin. His old habits were to be denied to a new way of life which included the totality of one's life — actions, words, and thoughts. Everything was to be subjected to Jesus. His standard was perfection. "Therefore you are to be perfect, as your heavenly Father is perfect" (Matthew 5:48). Jesus was not demanding a part-time or half-hearted commitment but wanted a complete devotion with Him as Lord of their lives. And Jesus never hid the cost involved in following Him. Some may have wanted to accept part of His teaching and claim the benefits which He promised, but were unwilling to commit to all that He commanded. But Jesus demanded a full commitment. C.S. Lewis compares Jesus to a dentist who does not only deal with the tooth causing a toothache but also works on all the other teeth which have not even begun to ache yet. He stated:

> "Dozens of people go to Him to be cured of some one particular sin which they are ashamed of . . . or which is obviously spoiling daily life (like bad temper or drunkenness). Well, He will cure it all right, but He will not stop there. That may be all you asked; but if once you call Him in, He will give the full treatment. That is why He warned people to 'count the cost' before becoming Christians."[1]

The perfection which Jesus desired is manifested in obedience. He required obedience of all who followed Him. "He who has my commandments and keeps them, he it is who loves Me; and he who loves Me shall be loved by My Father, and I will love him, and will disclose Myself to him" (John 14:21).

Jesus described this commitment in terms of a cross and self denial. "And He summoned the multitude with His disciples, and said to them, 'If anyone wishes to come after Me, let him deny himself, and take up his cross, and follow Me. For whoever wishes to save his life shall lose it; and whoever loses his life for My sake and the gospel's shall save it' " (Mark 8:34-35).

The message was plain and simple, but the cost was tremendous. He demanded the lives of His disciples, and that is all they had. The cost of discipleship presented the greatest barrier between Him and everyone following Him. His message was radical and it separated men. His message upset everyone. To the irreligious it caused them to give up all of their worldly values. To the religious it forced them to deny their traditions and spiritual pride and circumvent it all to Jesus. Many that heard the message of the cross decided that the price was too expensive.

Many people followed Jesus as long as He was giving free food by multiplying bread and fish. But when Jesus began to explain the commitment involved in following Him, they left as quickly as they had come. "As a result of this many of His disciples withdrew, and were not walking with Him anymore" (John 6:66). The former disciple said, "This is a difficult statement; who can listen to it?" (John 6:60).

Jesus never ran after a person who left and begged him to remain. Neither did He ever lower the cost to obtain a greater number of followers. He continually challenged men to follow Him, but He never forced a man to follow Him.

A young man came to Jesus with an intriguing question. He asked, "Teacher, what good thing shall I do that I may obtain eternal life?" (Matthew 19:16). Jesus responds to him to keep the commandments; the young man claims to have kept these commandments and asks, "What am I still lacking?" (Matthew 19:20). Jesus' reply to him was overwhelming. "Jesus said to him, 'If you wish to be complete, go and sell your possessions and give to the poor, and you shall have treasure in heaven; and come follow Me' " (Matthew 19:21). The answer to the young guy's search was discipleship; it was in following Jesus. This is what was truly missing in his life. But why does Jesus put His invitation in such drastic terms? Jesus, to avoid all misunderstandings, has to create an irrevocable situation from which there can be no retreat.

When he stands face to face with Jesus, it is the ultimate encounter. It is now a question of yes or no, a decision of obedience or disobedience.[2] "But when the young man heard this statement, he went away grieved; for he was one who owned much property" (Matthew 19:22).

The rich young ruler was not the only case where a would-be follower was presented with a demand that was more costly than anticipated. A scribe came to Jesus with the statement: " 'Teacher, I will follow you wherever you go.' And Jesus said to him, 'The foxes have holes, and the birds of the air have nests; but the Son of Man has nowhere to lay His head' " (Matthew 8:19-20). But Jesus would not let him negotiate his own contract. He said to another, "Follow Me; and allow the dead to bury their own dead" (Matthew 8:22). "And another also said, 'I will follow you, Lord; but first permit me to say good-bye to those at home' " (Luke 9:61). Jesus would never let someone set their own terms of discipleship. The man's statement was good until he added the word "but". If anyone ever came to Jesus with an "I will follow you Lord, but . . .", they would leave disappointed. No matter what the conditions were, whether legitimate or an excuse, Jesus set the terms. To this man Jesus said, "No one, after putting his hand to the plow and looking back, is fit for the kingdom of God" (Luke 9:62).

Not only did these examples have difficulty with the demands of Jesus, but some of the inner relationships did also. Peter denied Jesus three times after Jesus had predicted his rejection. The most striking of those who were not willing to go all the way was Judas. Judas, one of the twelve specially trained disciples, after following Him for three years, finally yielded to his greed and betrayed the Master. "And Judas Iscariot, who was one of the twelve, went off to the chief priests, in order to betray Him at an opportune time" (Mark 14:10-11).

Whatever Jesus was, He was not ordinary. He provoked extreme reactions, whether of acceptance or rejection. One moment they were all on His side, the next they were trying to lynch Him. And yet such was the authority of this extraordinary man that apparently He simply walked through a murderous crowd, and nobody laid a finger on him . . . He met enthusiastic acceptance, and bitter hostility; for it was hard to be neutral about Jesus. He drove people to extremes, and in so doing He divided them, deeply and irrevocably, into two opposing camps. "Anyone who is not for me, is really against me," He said; and conversely He told His followers that "Whoever is not against you is for you." But there does not seem to be much reason for neutral spectators.[3]

## CANNOT BE MY DISCIPLES

In John's gospel, there are three marks given for a disciple (as discussed in Chapter Two): abiding in the Word, loving one another, and bearing fruit. In the gospel of Luke are three negative comments regarding discipleship. Three times Jesus makes the statement that one "cannot be My disciple." All three of these passages are in Luke 14.

### More Than Family

Jesus taught that devotion to Him must be greater than even that to the family. "If anyone comes to Me, and does not hate his own father and mother and wife and children and brothers and sisters, yes, and even his own life, he cannot be My disciple" (Luke 14:26). In Luke 14, Jesus most graphically displays the immense cost of following Him. He teaches those who were going along with Him that to be His disciple one must obey Him even when it seems that it will cost him mother or father, wife (or husband), brother or sister, or children. Jesus gives two illustrations in this chapter which depict the cost of discipleship. In verses 28-30, He describes a man who begins to build a tower but because of a lack of funds is not able to complete it. He says that such a man would be ridiculed. Upon entering Seattle from the South on Interstate 5, one is stricken with the comical sight of

117

several freeway exits that end in mid-air. The unfinished ramps hanging in the middle of the air become a joke for all motorists who pass by. One wonders why they were not finished. Someone must have not adequately planned and calculated the cost of completion. Jesus is drawing a similar picture to teach His disciples not to begin something that they are not going to finish. Again He illustrates this point with the example of a king who goes to war. He says:

> "Or what king, when he sets out to meet another king in battle, will not first sit down and take counsel whether he is strong enough with ten thousand men to encounter the one coming against him with twenty thousand? Or else, while the other is still far away, he sends a delegation and asks terms of peace" (Luke 14:31-32).

Jesus once more is giving this lesson that if one wants to follow Him he must be ready to pay the price, and no human relationship can take precedent over Him.

### Carry His Cross

Sandwiched between the first "cannot be my disciple" and the two illustrations discussed previously is another charge to a would-be disciple. "Whoever does not carry his own cross and come after Me cannot be My disciple" (Luke 14:27). To follow after Jesus was to give up your life. When someone thought of the cross, he thought of an instrument of death. To take up a cross was similar to joining a funeral procession — one's own. It was a familiar sight in Roman Palestine to see a criminal on his way to execution, forced to carry his own cross. Even before Jesus gave Himself on the cross, the disciples knew what it meant to take up a cross. Discipleship was not for the squeamish or for people who were concerned about other people's opinions of them.[4]

Christ's call to follow Him was a call to absolute surrender, a self-death. "Christianity without self-death is only an abstract philosophy. It is Christianity without

118

Christ."[5] One of the biggest mistakes people make is to separate salvation from the lordship involved in being a disciple. Peter finished the first part of his sermon on the Day of Pentecost with this statement: "Therefore let all the house of Israel know for certain that God has made Him both Lord and Christ — this Jesus whom you crucified" (Acts 2:36). In this sermon Peter is acknowledging Jesus as both Lord and Christ. When the crowd thought of the Christ, they thought of the Messiah who would come to save them from their perils. Although Jesus was a different kind of Savior than they had anticipated, this is exactly what Peter is saying — Jesus is the Christ, the One who saves. But Peter referred to Jesus as more than the Christ. He prefaced Him with the title "Lord." Jesus was not only to be the Savior for the people, but also their Lord. A lord was a master. If Jesus is Lord, then He is the One who rules a person's life. Some people might want to accept Jesus as their Savior because they realize their lostness and want to be saved. But one cannot have Jesus as Savior unless he is prepared to put on Jesus as Lord. When the people believed Peter's sermon and were pierced in their hearts, they cried out, "Men and brethren, what shall we do?" (Acts 2:37). Peter's response was most emphatic. Not only did he tell them to be baptized as 3,000 were on that day, but he also told them to repent. To "repent" means to make an about face. It implies that one turns away from his old manner of life and turns to a new way of life. It involves a change of lords. Where one's self was the lord before, now Jesus is the lord of all facets of life. The command was to "repent and be baptized." Repentance preceded baptism because without it there is no change of lords, and as a result, no discipleship. Repentance and baptism go hand in hand, the same as Jesus being both Lord and Christ go hand in hand. The response of acknowledging Jesus as Lord and Christ and obeying by repenting and being baptized was forgiveness of sins and the gift of the Holy Spirit (Acts 2:38). A person cannot be a disciple or a Christian, in the true sense of the word, if Jesus is not lord of his life.

Paul spoke of the self-death to the Galatians: "I have been crucified with Christ; and it is no longer I who live, but Christ lives in me; and the life which I now live in the flesh I live by faith in the Son of God, who loved me, and delivered Himself up for me" (Galatians 2:20). Paul said to the Romans: "Or do you not know that all of us who have been baptized into Christ Jesus have been baptized into His death? Therefore we have been buried with Him through baptism into death, in order that as Christ was raised from the dead through the glory of the Father, so we too might walk in newness of life" (Romans 6:3-4).

Keith Phillips gives an interesting analogy concerning self death:

Let's suppose that on January 1, I was flying over Kansas when the plane exploded. My body fell to the ground and I was dead on impact. Before long a farmer discovered my corpse. There was no pulse, no heart-beat, no breath. My body was cold. Obviously I was dead. So the farmer dug a grave. But by the time he placed my body in the earth, it was too dark to cover it. Deciding he would finish in the morning, he returned home.

Then Christ came to me and said, "Keith, you are dead. Your life on this earth is over. But I will breathe into you a breath of new life if you promise to do anything I ask and go anywhere I send you."

My immediate reaction was, "No way! That's unreasonable. It's slavery." But then I realized I was not in a good bargaining position, and I quickly came to my senses. I wholeheartedly agreed.

Instantly my lungs, heart, and other vital organs began to function again. I came back to life. I was born again! From that point on no matter what Christ asked me to do or where He asked me to go, I was more than willing. No task was too difficult, no hours too long, no place too dangerous. Nothing was unreasonable. Why? Because I had no claim to my life. I was living on borrowed time,

Christ's time. Keith died on January 1 in a Kansas corn-field. Then I could say with Paul, "I have been crucified (have died) with Christ; and it is no longer (Keith) who is alive, but Christ (who) lives in me . . .⁶

Christ's call to take up a cross was a command to partake in His death and totally deny one's self in order to experience a new birth where one is totally committed to Him.

## Give Up Possessions

Jesus once more makes an uncompromising state-ment concerning discipleship: "So therefore, no one of you can be My disciple who does not give up all his own possessions" (Luke 14:33). Jesus had already taught those who were considering following that they could have no human relationship above Him. Now He is also instructing them that they cannot have any personal possession above Him. In fact, when Jesus is Lord, everything belongs to Him. This means that all posses-sions are given up to His Lordship. This might involve giving them up completely but it always means surren-dering them to the Lord in order for them to be used for His glory. As one's lifestyle relates to one's ultimate purpose so should one's possessions.

It seems curious that Jesus would demand such an extreme, but when the call of discipleship is analyzed it becomes evident that Jesus is producing an all or noth-ing situation. Dietrich Bonhoeffer explains the leaving of possessions this way:

If we would follow Jesus we must take certain definite steps. The first step, which follows the call, cuts the disciple off from his previous existence. The call to follow at once produces a new situation. To stay in the old situation makes discipleship impossible. Levi must leave the receipt of custom and Peter his nets in order to fol-low Jesus. One would have thought that nothing so drastic was necessary at such an early stage. Could not

Jesus have initiated the publican into some new religious experience, and leave them as they were before? He could have done so, had he not been the incarnate Son of God. But since He is the Christ, He must make it clear from the start that His Word is not an abstract doctrine, but the re-creation of the whole life of men. The only right and proper way is quite literally to go with Jesus. The call to follow implies that there is only one way of believing our Jesus Christ, and that is by leaving all and going with the incarnate Son of God.

The first step places the disciple in the situation where faith is possible. If he refuses to follow and stays behind, he does not know how to believe.[7]

The only way for Jesus' disciples to learn the way of faith is for them to plunge into absolute insecurity. If a disciple stays in his present situation, Jesus could be a help to him but He would not be Lord of all of his life. Jesus asks the disciple to give up all his possessions in order to create a new situation where it is possible to believe in Jesus. He creates a new situation where everything is staked completely in Him.[8] The cost is not only great, it is total. Because only as one surrenders completely to Jesus does one ever learn how to believe and become like Him.

The giving up of possessions is much like the man who responded to a destitute lady and gave her $20. Later after explaining her situation to his family, the family pooled their resources and came up with $100 which they decided to give her. The man went back to the lady and said, "Do you have the $20 that I gave you?" She replied, "Yes." "Then give it to me," he responded. She then reached into her pocket and gave the man back the $20. After receiving the $20, the man combined it with the $100, and gave it to her and said, "My family would like you to have this $120."[9]

This illustration is similar to discipleship. What little anyone has is merely resources entrusted to him by God. Therefore, when Christ calls a disciple to give up his possessions, he is simply asking him to return what really was not his in the first place. And similar to the story the end result of giving all to Jesus far outweighs the previous existence.

The barriers are high but the benefits are even greater.

"Jesus said, 'Truly I say to you, there is no one who has left house or brothers or sisters or mother or father or children or farms, for My sake and the gospel's sake, but that he shall receive a hundred times as much now in the present age, houses and brothers and sisters and mothers and children and farms, along with persecutions; and in the world to come eternal life' " (Mark 10: 29-30).

## QUESTIONS

1. Why did so many people choose not to follow Jesus?

2. What kind of commitment was Jesus trying to get His followers to make?

3. In Luke 14, Jesus says that one cannot be His disciple unless he does three things. What are these three things?

4. Do you have any personal relationships or possessions that are above Jesus? What are they?

5. What does it mean to have Jesus as "Lord" and "Savior"?

6. What is the relationship between "repentance" and "baptism"?

## FOOTNOTES

[1] C.S. Lewis, *Mere Christianity* (New York: MacMillan, 1943), pp. 171-172.

[2] Dietrich Bonhoeffer. *The Cost of Discipleship* (New York: Mac-Millan, 1963), pp. 83-84.

[3] R.T. France, *I Came to Set the Earth on Fire* (Downers Grove: Inter-Varsity Press, 1975), pp. 12-13.

[4] France, p. 58.

[5] Keith Phillips, *The Making of a Disciple* (Old Tappan: Fleming H. Revell, 1981), p. 17.

6 Phillips, pp. 18-19.

7 Dietrich Bonhoeffer. *The Cost of Discipleship* (New York: Mac-Millan, 1963), pp. 66-67.

8 Bonhoeffer, p. 68.

9 Walter A. Henrichsen, *Disciples Are Made — Not Born* (Wheaton: Victor, 1974), p. 29.

# BARRIERS
# TO
# DISCIPLESHIP

11

## OBSTACLES TODAY

In Jesus' day, the cost seemed to be in the forefront and the reason for a lack of discipleship was apparent — one simply was not willing to count the cost. However, in modern times the cost of discipleship and the plan of multiplying disciples seem to have been clouded in a mirage of religion. The basic reasons for a lack of making disciples are still the same as they were in Jesus' day. But it is good to examine churches and church leaders today to see how these barriers to discipleship are being manifested and also how they are being overcome. A survey was taken of 100 church leaders who were striving to have a ministry which multiplied disciples in order to obtain information on what is hindering churches today from fulfilling Jesus' plan. "Discipleship" was defined as it has been already in this study. There were many and various barriers to multiplying discipleship that were included in the survey, but two answers were overwhelmingly mentioned above others.

One of these reasons mentioned most frequently was that the concept of multiplying discipleship has not been taught effectively in churches and when it has, it has not been properly understood. This answer proved true in the survey itself. Many of the leaders surveyed did not understand the concept of multiplying discipleship themselves. When they were asked to relate barriers to multiplying discipleship, many answers reflect legitimate church problems but did not coincide with the specific nature of the lack of making multiplying disciples.

Ray Notgrass, a campus minister, stated his perception of the ignorance of the concept in the following manner:

> We simply haven't known the concept of multiplying by one teaching a few. It is something that we haven't pursued. It hasn't been seen as essential to the process of restoration or to the process of evangelism. It is something that has not been discussed, taught, or emphasized in our movement. We have usually had our emphasis on teaching and getting across the intellectual understanding of the truths of Scripture, especially certain "doctrines" and teachings that identify our movement, but we have had little emphasis on seeking to apply those principles and developing lives of discipleship.[1]

W. Gregg Strawn, a minister, stated: "The fact that multiplying discipleship has been a very uncommon teaching in churches of Christ has been a barrier to its practice. Most felt that 'getting people in the water' was all that really mattered and that even that wasn't their job."[2] Others added that this concept may be understood only on the cognitive level but not to the extent that it can be applied. Marty Fuqua, a minister, comments: "The older Christian may understand the 'principle' of 'Multiplying Discipleship,' but he may not understand the 'practicals' of how to help the young convert."[3] Ken Ball, a church leader, added this viewpoint:

> Christians lack the insight into how the Lord's Great Command applies to them personally. They are aware of the command to make disciples; they understand what it means, but they cannot see themselves doing it. Consequently, they fail to make the decision to try, and in failing to try they fail to appropriate God's empowerment to get the job done. Even though many would admit

it is proper to really get involved in discipling, they simply do not decide to get "off the dime." Traditional ways of doing things die hard. Although Christ is the epitome of one who invested an extended period of His life to the discipling of a few (12), the modern church seems to have overlooked Christ's method. "Legitimate" methods have been mass meetings, and cottage classes that lead as far as conversion.[4]

The other reason most frequently given as an obstacle to multiplying discipleship had to do with a lack of examples to imitate among leaders, especially elders and a pattern in the church which has not actively made disciples, and as a result, most older Christians are set in a mold of non-discipling which does not give the younger Christians an example to follow and causes a stumbling block for discipleship at the present time. it was mentioned that this lack of leadership among leaders was because no one had discipled them.

A preacher, Stanley Sherman, believes that the biggest barriers to discipleship in churches are "the examples of non-involvement and sensed non-interest on the part of older church members."[5] Tom Torpy, a minister, saw as the biggest problem the lack of "deeply spiritual leadership (especially the gray-headed men of faith)."[6] He also states, "Christian men and women will profit by having older role models to imitate. Spiritual leaders must become our heroes."[7] Steve Sapp, a campus minister, says, "There are very few examples of this process in older Christians (especially those in leadership roles). This makes it more difficult to disciple new converts because they don't see 'older' Christians doing it."[8]

Tom Yoakum, a Bible instructor, also commented on this problem:

Elders and local preachers (if this approach to discipling is introduced by a "second minister") view this as a threat to their leadership. Someone is coming in to establish a "power base" with their group of people who are carbon copies of the discipling minister or of the place where he has trained.[9]

Ray Notgrass places part of the blame on the attitudes and practices of preachers.

There has been a tendency for preachers to do everything and not delegate responsibilities to others (and we have often been willing for preachers to do it all!). There has been the tendency for preachers to go for the big splash, to go for quick numbers by trying to baptize as many people as possible with little effort at nurturing. There is also the tendency for preachers not to be open with their own lives to others, a necessity in multiplying discipleship.[10]

There were some other barriers included in the survey which deserve mention. Among these were misplaced priorities by Christians, the lack of concentrating on a few, the desire for immediate results, the failure to create the fellowship and Christian community of the New Testament church, a lack of commitment, an unwillingness to devote sufficient time and a difficulty in changing past traditions.[11]


# OVERCOMING OBSTACLES

In overcoming these various obstacles to multiplying discipleship, these church leaders responded in the survey with many suggestions for overcoming barriers. Of the ideas submitted, two answers appeared more than others, and these two correspond to the two obstacles discussed previously.

First, it was emphasized that a greater biblical teaching must take place in churches concerning discipleship and especially in regard to the life of Jesus. These leaders also realized the necessity of going back to the example of Jesus discipling the twelve and emulating His example in our present day churches.[12]

Ray Notgrass said concerning teaching the life of Jesus that the church needs to:

> Focus more on the life and ministry of Jesus in our teaching and preaching in the church instead of having a major emphasis on intellectualizing, atomizing, and using as proof texts the doctrines and instructions given by Paul. We have to be centered on Jesus to remain connected to the Head.[13]

Tom Yoakum stated that it is necessary for the church to:

> Establish the Biblical basis of this approach from Christ's personal ministry out of the Scriptures themselves and also the apostolic examples in Paul and his coworkers. Using "discipling manuals" sparingly and with concern to weed out unbiblical concepts[14]

When the example and plan of Jesus is taught from God's Word in both a public and private manner, the problem of a lack of understanding of the discipling concept could be eliminated, and more people would be motivated to make disciples.[15]

The second suggestion for overcoming obstacles was for someone who understood the concept actually to start discipling a few. It was suggested that it would be good if it were a minister or someone working full time for the church. However, it was also emphasized that the concept must include more than just full time church workers. A division in discipling among "clergy" and "laity" is actually part of the problem as was observed among those surveyed. If the elders were not qualified to disciple, discipleship still should take place through the leadership of someone. It was also expressed that people of all ages, especially those who are older, should be discipled.

Tom Reynolds, a minister, suggests to "start small with high quality. Have the minister take a lot of time and train two or three men who will then train two or

three men. Don't assume the elders are qualified."[16]
Charles Stelding, a Bible instructor, makes a similar observation — "In a church where no real discipleship has taken place, the minister can initiate this task among a few. A mere 'class' will not be adequate."[17] Mike Buckley makes the following suggestion:

> Ephesians 4:11-13 states that leaders must equip the saints. If the elders and ministers can't equip the saints then another evangelist should come and train these men to understand the concept of discipleship. Men should learn to equip/train their own families. Small groups should be used within the church to shepherd/train each other. Older Christians should choose a few less mature Christians to help them develop.[18]

Ken Ball offers the following solution:

> Someone who is actively engaged in converting people must make a special effort to be with those prospective soul-winners to guide them in an "on-the-job" experience. The Mormons have a great deal of success with this technique. Perhaps this is why the Lord sent the disciples out two-by-two. In other words someone has to take the lead in discipling the prospective disciplers. This will require a lot of perseverance on the part of those willing to take the lead.

> Although it will likely be a slow process, the church will have to observe the Lord's discipling process being successful in a modern-day setting. So, a small group of dedicated men are going to have to set a successful example. In the meantime, those who are willing, and who can, are going to have to find others who are willing to become disciplers and work with them. It doesn't seem likely to me that a whole lot of people are going to jump on something that is not exactly a "bandwagon" yet. Once it becomes one, the process could snow-ball into a very fruitful experience for the church.[19]

Several other suggestions were made which also would help discipleship in churches. Among these were internship programs, a greater commitment, sending

Christians to places that are successful in discipling, teaching life-style evangelism, greater training for preachers in discipleship, allowing the preachers more time for discipling, focusing on a few, and ministers staying longer in one location.

In summary, the barriers to discipleship have not changed drastically from the first century. And the way to overcome the barriers today can only happen the way it did in the first century with an obedience to the commands of Jesus.

## QUESTIONS

1. What are some of the barriers to multiplying discipleship that were suggested by these church leaders? Which two were prevalent?

2. What are some barriers which you see?

3. What suggestions did these church leaders make which need to be implemented in your life and that of your congregation?

4. What suggestions can you make which will help us to overcome these obstacles in discipleship?

## FOOTNOTES

[1] Survey on Discipleship, information collected by Milton Jones January, 1982.

[2] through [19] *Ibid.*

# SELECTION
# IS
# THE KEY

# 12

**A**s has been mentioned previously, there are only a few people anyone can disciple at one time. Since a person only has twenty-four hours in a day and this is the only life one has to count for something, it is crucial that the people whom one chooses to disciple are the right ones.

Selection is one of the greatest keys in making disciples. The key for good cooking is selecting the proper ingredients, and this same principle applies in selecting among many people the few whom one will disciple. In Jesus' ministry there were many who were following Him. Many of these followers were sincere and obedient. In Luke 10, there were seventy followers, but out of these, He selected twelve for special training. In churches today, there are many good people all of whom need discipling but because of limited time and the nature of discipleship, only a few can be chosen at any one time by any one person. Therefore, there must be selection.

Jesus' greatest concern was for quality, not quantity. He wanted to reach the masses, but He knew this would only happen as He fully trained a few. Waylon Moore states: "A decision that our ministry will be intensive rather than extensive will change our whole life. Quality begets quantity. It takes vision to disciple a man to reach the mass. If you train one man then you penetrate the multitude."[1]

Since there is a limited number of people one can disciple, there is the necessity of selection. However, this does not mean that there is exclusion of other Christians. As mentioned in Chapter Seven, there need to be good relationships on all levels — both the intimate and the distant levels. There is only exclusion when bad relationships exist on the outer levels. But there will never be relationships on the inner levels where discipleship occurs unless people are selected for these levels.

If selection must take place, then disciples need to know the qualities for which to look in a disciple, how to choose the disciple, and what to do with the disciple once he is selected. The following information applies specifically to those intimate levels of relationship and especially applies to those chosen for levels one and two.

## WHAT TO LOOK FOR

The men Jesus selected to train were ordinary men. They came from ordinary walks of life — fishermen, tax-collectors, and others similar to them. The men whom Jesus called appear to be different from what most people would expect. These people hardly seem to be the type of people whom a business would select for top management positions. Not only were they ordinary men, but they were also individuals. They were not all alike. Simon the Zealot hated the Romans who occupied Palestine, and Matthew the tax-collector worked for them. The people whom Jesus chose were not only unlikely choices in themselves, but even more so as a lot.

Jesus, though, had the unique ability to see the possibilities in a person. He did not merely see them as they were, but he visualized what they could become by God's power. When choosing a disciple today, the discipler must be careful not to choose according to the world's standards but according to God's. Therefore, everyone who is discipled should not necessarily be alike in temperament, personality, or aptitude. God loves variety. The discipler must be like Jesus and see the potential in a person when that person is fully trained. A discipler must never forget that God is in the business of changing people. The impetuous fisherman, Peter, hardly seemed a likely choice to become a leader in the early church, but Jesus saw the possibilities in him from the beginning. Jesus said to him, "You are Simon the Son of John; you shall be called Cephas" (John 1:42). Jesus saw in this shaky, fallible fisherman named Simon many possibilities, and he gave him a new name, Rock, which is what he was to become.

It does not take long to find weaknesses and inadequacies in any human being. As a result, perfection cannot be the quality for which the discipler is looking. God seems to have a habit of choosing unlikely people to fulfill his tasks. It seems that He delights in selecting someone without the natural leadership qualities.

In the Old Testament, many of the great leaders of faith were unlikely candidates and felt quite inadequate for the roles for which they had been selected. When God called Moses to deliver the people of Israel out of Egyptian bondage, he in no way felt up to the task. "But Moses said to God, 'Who am I, that I should go to Pharoah, and that I should bring the sons of Israel out of Egypt?' " (Exodus 3:11). Gideon had similar feelings of inadequacy. When God sent him to deliver Israel from the hand of Midian, Gideon only came up with excuses. "And he said to Him, 'O Lord, how shall I deliver Israel? Behold, my family is the least in Manasseh, and I am the youngest in my father's house' " (Judges 6:15). When God called Jeremiah to be a prophet to go to the nations, he also believed God had the wrong number. "Then I said, 'Alas, Lord God! Behold, I do not know how to speak, because I am a youth' " (Jeremiah 1:6). In all three examples of these Old Testament leaders, they responded to God's call with excuses of inadequacy. But in all three cases of inadequacy, God responded to them to show that He was adequate, and their adequacy would rest in Him. To Moses, "He said, 'Certainly I will be with you' " (Exodus 3:12). In Gideon's case, "the Lord said to him, 'Surely I will be with you' " (Judges 6:16). God spoke to Jeremiah and said, "For I am with you to deliver you" (Jeremiah 1:8).

God's presence makes up for inadequacies. How does this relate to making disciples? It is in this very act of making disciples that Jesus promises once again, "and lo, I am with you always" (Matthew 28:20). This means that God is not only at work fulfilling the inadequacies of people being discipled, but also assisting in the inadequacies of the discipler in his selection process.

Jesus was not the only New Testament character who chose unlikely people to disciple. Barnabas, that champion disciple maker in the book of Acts, chose two people whom no one else wanted. Barnabas chose Paul when everyone was either afraid of him or did not trust him. He also chose John Mark when Paul wanted to give up on him because of his quitting on the first missionary journey.

Paul followed in the footsteps of Barnabas when he chose Timothy to disciple. The picture painted of Timothy does not readily appear to have the marks of leadership. Timothy appeared to be timid and afraid: "Now if Timothy comes, see that he is with you without cause to be afraid" (1 Corinthians 16:10). He also was very young and not the management type: "Let no one look down on your youthfulness" (1 Timothy 4:12). Health also was not one of Timothy's strong points. He might have been one of those people who was always getting sick: "No longer drink water exclusively, but use a little wine for the sake of your stomach and your frequent ailments" (1 Timothy 5:23). Timothy might have also needed to appear more dignified to be a leader. Perhaps he came across as very emotional or subjective: "Recalling your tears, I long to see you" (2 Timothy 1:4, NIV). Risk-taking also seemed to be a leadership quality Timothy did not possess: "For God has not given us a spirit of timidity, but of power and love and discipline" (2 Timothy 1:7). It also seemed that Timothy was rather immature: "Now flee from youthful lusts" (2 Timothy 2:22).[2] In spite of all these apparent strikes against him, Timothy was a good choice for selection.

God has in the past used people like Timothy for His kingdom rather than all the natural-born leaders, and He will probably continue to do so in today's world. Paul explained the reason for this peculiar selection to the Corinthians:

> "God has chosen the foolish things of the world to shame the wise, and God has chosen the weak things of the world to shame the things which are strong, and the base things of the world and the despised, God has chosen, the things that are not, that He might nullify the things that are, that no man should boast before God" (1 Corinthians 1:27-29).

Although disciples can be certain that God is with them in the selection process and that many characteristics that are important to man are not to God, there are some important qualities that the Bible teaches for which to look in selecting someone to disciple.

### Reliable

"Now it is required that those who have been given a trust must prove faithful" (1 Corinthians 4:2, NIV). If one had to have a bottom line requirement for selecting a disciple, it would be faithfulness.

The primary quality that Paul teaches Timothy to look for in someone to disciple in the multiplying verse, 2 Timothy 2:2, is "faithfulness." The New International Version says that this person is to be "reliable." If there was any one characteristic for which Timothy was to look it was whether or not a person was faithful or reliable. If this person is given a job, will he see it through? If there was any quality that Timothy possessed above others it was in his faithfulness. "For this reason I have sent to you Timothy, who is my beloved and faithful child in the Lord" (1 Corinthians 4:15). Paul again commends his faith in his last letter to him: "For I am mindful of the sincere faith within you" (1 Timothy 1:5). Paul had a high regard for faithfulness and stick-to-itiveness.[3]

The people who most disturbed Paul were people who quit or turned back. John Mark's failure to finish caused him to break up his relationship with the one who discipled him. He also showed his displeasure with Demas: "For Demas, having loved this present world, has deserted me and gone to Thessalonica" (2 Timothy 4:10). Concerning his Roman trial, Paul said, "At my first defense no one supported me, but all deserted me" (2 Timothy 4:16).

Timothy may have had his problems and weaknesses, but he was not a quitter. He was faithful, and as Paul taught Timothy to train leaders to take his place, he advised first of all that they be faithful, trustworthy, and reliable men.[4]

In his parable of the money, Jesus told of the master who commended the good slave because he had been faithful (Luke 19:17). He again teaches the importance of reliability by stating, "He who is faithful in a very little thing is faithful also in much; and he who is unrighteous in a very little thing is unrighteous also in much" (Luke 16:10).

In today's age, where people have short attention spans and tend to stick with something only while it is a fad or when it feels good, the quality of faithfulness is eminently needed in the selection of disciples. Allen Hadidian emphasizes greatly this characteristic of faithfulness:

Listen discipler. Do not pour your life into someone

138

who is inconsistent in doing assignments or fulfilling little responsibilities, or who shows other signs of unfaithfulness. Be careful about giving up on someone, however. There will be times periodically when a person will stumble in this area. The person to look out for is the one whose life is characterized by irresponsibility and unfaithfulness. Do not commit yourself to a discipling relationship with that kind of person. It may be that you will want to spend some time with him in talking through his problem and how he can overcome it. That might be a wise thing to do. But when it comes to selecting your "Timothy," find a person whose life is characterized by faithfulness. It has been my experience that if a person has a teachable attitude and a heart for God, he will not have any problem with being faithful.[5]

### Worker

Timothy could not only be described as a faithful person, but he was also known to be a hard worker. "We sent Timothy, our brother and God's fellow-worker" (1 Thessalonians 3:2). In Romans 16:21, Paul called Timothy, "my workfellow."

When Jesus called his followers, He did not call sunbathers on the Sea of Galilee but fishermen who were mending their nets. God always uses the hard worker. Therefore, when selection is made for disciples, one should look for the person who is eager to work harder longer.[6]

### Learner

Inherent in the very word "disciple" is a learner. As a result, anyone who is selected should be one who is willing to learn. He should possess the willingness to submit to being taught. Not only should he be willing to be taught, but he must be willing also to be taught by the person who is discipling him. One can observe whether a person is teachable by how many questions he asks and the desire to find the true answers. A disciple is always studying to learn more and more of God's truth. He will never get enough. Many church workers view themselves as analysts of the church and love to criticize people for weaknesses or merely critique sermons and lessons. One with a teachable spirit does not seek to be a critic but is trying to learn from every person and every lesson.

### Hunger

The prophet Isaiah stated: "And if you give yourself to the hungry, and satisfy the desire of the afflicted, then your light will rise in darkness, and your gloom will become like midday" (Isaiah 58:10). People who are selected to be discipled should have a hunger. This hunger may be seen in three areas: a hunger to be involved in a disciple-making ministry, a hunger for God, and hunger to pay any price.[7]

The person selected should have hunger to become a discipler. Some church members want to learn to a certain extent but do not yet have the desire to share and disciple others. If a disciple is devoting his life to someone, he needs to be confident that this relationship will reproduce. Therefore, selection should be made among people who are eager to be a part of a multiplying ministry.

The one selected should have a hunger for God. Paul spoke of his desire to know Jesus — "that I may know Him, and the power of His resurrection and the fellowship of His sufferings, being conformed to His death" (Philippians 3:10). God has said, "Let not a wise man boast of his wisdom, and let not the mighty man boast of his might, let not a rich man boast of his riches; but let him who boasts boast of this, that he understands and knows Me" (Jeremiah 9:23-24). This person will desire God's Word like he desires food. He will read, study, and memorize the Scriptures. Not only will he listen to God's Word, but he will also consistently communicate with God in prayer. His life will show that he is concerned with the things of God and wants to live more for Him than himself. "As the deer pants for the water brooks, so my soul pants for Thee, O God" (Psalm 42:1).

The disciple should also have a hunger to pay any price. Jesus' twelve were willing to leave their homes and occupations to follow Him. Jesus always gave the cost: "If anyone would come after me, he must deny himself and take up his cross daily and follow me" (Luke 9:23). Jesus gave the challenge of discipleship and allowed people to respond. He did not force anyone to follow Him. The kind of person who followed Him knew that time, money, and his life were not his own.

## Submissive

For one to be discipled, he must have a submissive spirit. He should have this submission in every area of his life. Most of all he is to submit to the authority of Christ, obeying Him in all aspects. He also should be submissive to all authorities to whom God has delegated authority whether it be civil authority or leaders in the church. His submission should be voluntary and out of joy. He must be submissive to the one who is to disciple him. This means that he should be vulnerable and transparent to his discipler respecting his maturity. If an air of competitiveness occurs, it will be difficult to disciple the individual. Many people today have the philosophy of "do your own thing." This kind of independent spirit will never accomplish the will of God.

## Discipline

A disciple is a disciplined person. The apostle Paul compares the life of a disciple to the discipline of an athlete.

> "Do you not know that those who run in a race all run, but only one receives the prize? Run in such a way that you may win. And everyone who competes in the games exercises self-control in all things. They then do it to receive a perishable wreath, but we an imperishable. Therefore, I run in such a way as not without aim; I box in

such a way, as not beating the air; but I buffet my body
and make it my slave, lest possibly, after I have preached
to others, I myself should be disqualified" (1 Corinthians
9:24-27).

Some may think that the spiritual life is mystical and
opposed to the structured or disciplined life. Paul
teaches the contrary. He states, "discipline yourself for
the purpose of godliness" (1 Timothy 4:7).

Modern man has been flooded with a life of self-
indulgence. His way has become unrelated, nondirected,
and without self-control. The only remedy is discipline.
"To the Christian, discipline means discipleship — following Jesus, with one's self denied and one's cross resolutely carried."[8] Walter Henrichsen emphasizes the life
of discipline:

> It is evident that one does not become a "faithful per-
> son" by being a week-end Christian. The faithful person
> is one who has applied the Scriptures to every area of his
> life. The life of discipleship is a life of discipline — the two
> words come from the same root . . . . The gold medal
> goes to the athlete who has learned how to discipline
> himself, who has learned to say no to the myriad dis-
> tractions that cross a person's life, who has a clear-cut
> objective and has resolved in his soul to stay with it until
> he accomplishes it. This is the kind of person God uses.[9]

## Gender

Discipling involves an intensive fellowship where much
time is spent together over a long period of time. Since
discipling requires vulnerability and openness in all areas
of life, there would be many limitations in discipling
someone of the opposite sex. Discipling, as discussed in
this study, would be unadvised between people of the
opposite sex (especially on levels one and two). This
does not mean that one does not minister to people of
the opposite sex. Everyone in the body of Christ ministers to everyone else, but discipling should occur
among people of the same sex. All the discipling exam-

ples that have been studied (Jesus and the twelve, Barnabas and Paul, Paul and Timothy, etc.) have been of people of the same sex. If someone of the opposite sex wants to be discipled, the best thing to do is to lead that person to someone of his (or her) sex.[10]

### Available

A person may have all the above qualities and even more, but if he is unable to find the time to devote to being discipled, it will be impossible to have a discipling relationship. Discipling takes a great deal of time. Jesus invested a great deal of time in the lives of a few men. Therefore, this person must be one who is willing to devote time to this relationship in order to be trained.

### Whom You Want

There is one more point that is often overlooked. In nearly every church, a disciple maker could look around and find more people that he could possibly disciple. There may be many more people with the qualities already mentioned than he could disciple. After preparing himself spiritually and examining people in light of the Word, how does one finally decide whom to choose? Jesus' call of the twelve sheds light on this question. "And He went up to the mountain and summoned those whom He Himself wanted" (Mark 3:13). After all the preliminaries had been taken care of, Jesus chose whom He wanted. Someone finally has to be selected for discipleship to ever take place. After someone has studied God's plan for discipleship, examined the prospective person for the qualities mentioned previously, and prayed about it; he finally must make a decision, and this is where this last point comes into focus — he chooses whom he wants. Choosing whom you want is not where a disciple maker starts but ends. After seeking God's will and relying on His guidance, the disciple maker's choice should not only be what he wants but also in harmony with what God wants. Ultimately the whole relationship is in God's hands, but God requires men to take action and select.

## HOW TO CHOOSE

It has been discussed what qualities should be sought after in choosing a person to disciple, but how does the actual selection take place?

### Prayer

Before selection of the twelve, Jesus spent much time in prayer. During all of His ministry, Jesus prayed, but He especially wanted to pray about this decision because of the magnitude of entrusting his ministry to such a few people.

> "And it was at this time that He went off to the mountain to pray, and He spent the whole night in prayer to God. And when day came, He called His disciples to Him; and chose twelve of them, whom He also named as apostles" (Luke 6:12-13).

Jesus' decision was based upon a careful process of close observation and diligent prayer. He was careful not to make a hasty selection. After observation, a disciple maker should commit himself to intensive prayer asking for God's direction in the selection.

### Initiating the Selection

After personal observation and prayer, the person selected must be actually invited to be discipled. Jesus called His disciples personally. "Did I myself not choose you, the twelve, and yet one of you is a devil?" (John 6:10). Upon issuing the invitation, the discipler should explain how he was led to select him — by close personal observation of the qualities of his life and prayer. He should then fully explain the relationship involved in discipling. The commitment involved in this relationship should also be explained along with the submission that will need to take place to the discipler. The discipler should also communicate to him the vision for multiplying disciples in order to win the world to Christ and how

144

he fits into this picture. Although the discipler initiates the invitation, the potential disciple should be allowed to decide himself.[11] Jesus never begged anyone to follow Him or forced anyone. He always gave them the free choice to make a decision, and this should also occur in discipling relationships today.

## WHAT TO DO

In deciding what to teach a person once he is selected to disciple, one could draw up an extensive curriculum showing in detail particular teachings and doctrines that should be learned. Various teaching methods and when to teach each of the specifics could also be explored and itemized. However, this study will look at the teaching method on a more general manner in three aspects.

### Be With Him

After Jesus had summoned those whom He wanted, He then "appointed twelve, that they might be with Him" (Mark 3:14). Jesus' greatest teaching method was that He imparted Himself. He spent time with His disciples. He was with them in all types of situations, among all types of people, and in various places. Probably the most effective teaching one can do today in discipling is to spend time with a person in all situations. This will include formal situations like a class or a discipler group meeting. It will include some regularly scheduled times for prayer and sharing. Some of the time will naturally be scheduled for planned evangelistic activites. But much of the time will include some of that informal teaching as one is traveling to a destination, eating together, or going to a social event. The disciples must learn how to function in all types of situations. Therefore the discipler must devote time to be with him in all types of situations. When one analyzes the way a child is raised in a family, it is evident that most of the child's education does not take place in a formal situation. The child learns by listening and questioning as natural events occur around him.

Jesus uses this fundamental educational concept of the family as his method of discipling. In fact, Paul calls Timothy his "beloved son" (1 Corinthians 4:17) and refers to himself as a "father through the gospel" to the Corinthians (1 Corinthians 4:15). Discipling will not take place unless the discipler chooses to be with the person he is discipling.

### Send Them Out to Preach

It is not good enough merely to impart knowledge, the knowledge must be applied. The disciple is to become like Jesus in his actions. Jesus not only spent time with them teaching and imparting His life, but He also delegated responsibility to them and commissioned them to do the things He was doing. "And He appointed twelve, that they might be with Him, and that He might send them out to preach" (Mark 3:14). Jesus was not only with the disciples, but He also sent them out to preach as He had been doing. "And He summoned the twelve and began to send them out in pairs; and He was giving them authority over the unclean spirits" (Mark 6:7). Jesus sent them out, and they obeyed Him. "And they went out and preached that man should repent. And they were casting out many demons and were annointing with oil many sick people and healing them" (Mark 6:12-12). After going out, the disciples returned and reported to Him for supervision and to learn how to be even more effective the next time. "And the apostles gathered together with Jesus; and they reported to Him all they had done and taught" (Mark 6:30). A person can never truly become a learner without experience — to be encouraged by victories and persevere through mistakes. One only develops character through experience, and education is only fruitful when it is practical. Jesus gave them something to do because they needed to learn through experience. And what better activity could He give them to do than what He was already doing? They had seen Him do it, now it was their turn. A discipler today needs to follow the pattern of Jesus. He must allow the people he is discipling to learn through experience. He needs to give them a job to do — send them out to preach. A discipler will get them to do the same things that He has been doing. By doing this, he has a pattern to follow and someone to whom he may turn for valuable counsel.

### And the Things You Have Heard From Me

"And the things which you have heard from me in the presence of many witnesses, these entrust to faithful men, who will be able to teach others also" (2 Timothy 2:2). Paul describes his discipling curriculum in this multiplying passage as "these things". What then are "these things" and the basic curriculum to be imparted? "These things" really represent all that Paul knows. Paul imparted to Timothy all that he possibly could; he had devoted his life to training him. This is really the curriculum for a discipler — all he knows about Jesus and how to walk in Him. The discipler cannot do any more than to continually teach the person he is discipling all that he knows and is learning about the Lord. By doing so, he is imparting himself.

## QUESTIONS

1. Why does God often choose unlikely people for His tasks?
2. What is it that makes up for our inadequacies in God's mission for us?
3. Who are some unlikely people in the Bible who were chosen for a particular purpose?
4. What are some important qualities to look for in selecting someone to disciple?
5. How should the selection actually take place?
6. What should you do with the disciple once he has been selected?

# FOOTNOTES

1 Waylon B. Moore, *New Testament Follow-Up: For Pastors and Laymen* (Grand Rapids: Eerdmans, 1963), p. 68.

2 William J. Petersen, *The Discipling of Timothy* (Wheaton: Victor, 1980), pp. 176-177.

3 *Ibid.* p. 177.

4 *Ibid.* p. 178.

5 Allen Hadidian, *Successful Discipling* (Chicago: Moody Press, 1979), pp. 86-87.

6 Eims, *The Lost Art of Disciple Making*, p. 130.

7 *Ibid.* pp. 90-91.

8 Richard Shelley Taylor, *The Disciplined Life* (Minneapolis: Dimension, 1962), p. 26.

9 Henrichsen, pp. 17-18.

10 Hadidian, pp. 84-85.

11 Keith Phillips, *The Making of a Disciple* (Old Tappan: Fleming H. Revell, 1981), p. 99.

# SOME CONCLUDING THOUGHTS

# 13

Although Christians have been perplexed by the Great Commission and many have considered it an impossibility, there is a way to do it. It is Jesus' way — making disciples. With a greater understanding of the concept of multiplying discipleship, it is possible for churches today to launch out in new dimensions of effectiveness.

Churches can search for methods in order to win people to Christ, but the only method that indeed can multiply the work force in order to get the job done is this plan of making disciples. There have been other schemes and there will be others in the future, but the one that works is still the original.

It has been seen that the grand evangelistic methods of most churches today have not won the world. And it is apparent that churches must be doing more than mere evangelism if the impact is to be made on all the world. Jesus concentrated His ministry on the development and training of a few in order to reach the masses. If the masses are to be reached today, it will begin with a few people being discipled in the manner of Jesus.

In order for the process of making disciples to begin, there must first be some true disciples. It is imperative for churches today to be teaching the truth of what it means to be a disciple ( $\mu\alpha\theta\eta\tau\dot{\eta}s$ ). Until Christians are truly conforming their minds, actions, and words, to that of Jesus; it will be impossible to fulfill the Great Commission. The reason that churches have not been making disciples is that they have been reproducing after their own kind, and their own kind have not been true disciples like Jesus. In order to begin, there must be disciples who are more than pupils but learners of the Master in every area of their life.

Once churches are seriously teaching the marks of a disciple (abiding in the Word, loving one another, and bearing fruit) and practicing them; then and only then can they be effective in making other disciples in a process that not only evangelizes people but also edifies and equips them.

The process of discipling cannot start big; it must begin in the manner of Jesus and in the instruction of Paul's charge to Timothy in 2 Timothy 2:2. As Jesus and others who followed Him concentrated on a reliable few and imparted their lives to those disciples teaching them to observe all things, the church today needs to follow similar suit. The evangelistic programs and campaigns that have been tried in the past will not get the job done — the only way to accomplish the task is to have a plan that multiplies the workers.

When a few disciples are trained who will be able to train others and still others, the number of disciples can increase at a geometric ratio. Although it begins with a nominal amount of people, it has been shown that with only a few reliable people the world could be won within a minimal number of years. This is where Jesus devoted His three years of ministry, and it is what was exemplified in the book of Acts with His disciples. During those early years, the disciples multiplied throughout all the world. It can happen again, but only if Christians have the same lifestyle, commitment, and plan for making disciples.

In order to accomplish these same results, churches will need to have ministries which have all four phases of the four phase following. Their ministries will need to reach the pool of humanity, provide evangelistic activities, confront people personally with God's Word, and train Christians to reproduce and multiply.

Not only will disciples need to follow that four phase following, but they will also need to have good relationships at all six levels which Jesus had. For discipleship to occur which will multiply to all the world, Christians must devote much time to developing relationships on levels one, two, and three. Only as intimate relationships develop among Christians will disciples be trained who will be equipped to multiply.

These disciples will develop a whole new way of thinking where everything in their lives (actions, words, and thoughts) relate to their ultimate objective of glorifying God. These disciples will be glorifying God in their relationship to Him and their relationships with other people. The way of discipleship becomes more than just an activity; it is a lifestyle.

The life of Jesus is not an easy way. When Jesus called a man to follow Him, He demonstrated an absolute surrender of His life. The cost was total then, and it must be for disciples today. Otherwise, there will be no hope for multiplication. Jesus only uses those who are totally surrendered to Him and are not making their own conditions for discipleship. There are many barriers to discipleship that exist in churches today, but these can be overcome with an obedience to the commands of discipleship which Jesus originally instituted. The cost of following Jesus was great then, and it is now; but the benefits of going with Jesus have always far outweighed the cost.

Ultimately, for discipleship to occur, it will take some learners of Jesus to make the commitment to devote their lives to discipling a few men who will be able to teach others. For this to occur, there must be a selection. There are multitudes of people in the world, but a disciple maker can only impart his life in Christ to a few. Since a person can only disciple a few people in his life and he wants his life to count for something, selection is most important and must be done according to guidelines set in the New Testament.

The time to act is now. Jesus said: "Go therefore and make disciples of all the nations baptizing them in the name of the Father and the Son and the Holy Spirit" (Matthew 28:19). Jesus' command can be done, must be done, and will be done as churches today make true disciples who will multiply throughout all the world.

## QUESTIONS

1. After making this study what do you think is the best method for winning people to Christ?

2. How can this be enacted in your congregation?

3. Who are some people you know that need discipling?

4. Who are some church leaders to whom you can teach this concept?

5. What are you going to do about making disciples?

# BIBLIOGRAPHY

a Kempis, Thomas. *Of the Imitation of Christ*. Springdale: Whitaker, House, 1981.

Allee, John Gage, ed. *Webster's Encyclopedia of Dictionaries*, New York: Ottenheimer, 1978.

Barclay, William. *The Letters to the Galatians and Ephesians*. Philadelphia: Westminister, 1958.

Barclay, William. *The Mind of Jesus*. New York: Harper and Row, 1960.

Barnhouse, Donald Grey. *The Love Life*. Glendale: Regal, 1973.

Bender, Urie. *The Witness*. Scottdale: Herald Press, 1965.

The Bible, King James Version.

The Bible, New American Standard Version.

The Bible, New International Version.

Bonhoeffer, Dietrich. *The Cost of Discipleship*. New York: MacMillan, 1959.

Bruce, A.B. *The Training of the Twelve*. New Canaan: Keats, 1979.

Carrol, Lewis. *Alice in Wonderland*. New York: Peebles, n.d.

Coleman, Robert E. *The Master Plan of Evangelism*. Old Tappan: Fleming H. Revell, 1973.

Coleman, Robert E. *They Meet the Master*. Old Tappan: Fleming H. Revell, 1973.

Collins, Gary. *How to Be a People Helper*. Santa Ana Vision House, 1976.

Cosgrove, Francis M., Jr. *Essentials of Discipleship*. Colorado Springs: Navpress, 1980.

Eims, Leroy. *Be the Leader You Were Meant to Be*. Wheaton: Victor, 1975.

Eims, Leroy. *Disciples in Action*. Wheaton: Victor, 1981.

Eims, Leroy. *The Lost Art of Disciple Making*. Grand Rapids: Zondervan, 1978.

Eims, Leroy. *What Every Christian Should Know About Growing.* Wheaton: Victor, 1976.

Engel, James F., and H. Wilbert Norton. *What's Gone Wrong with the Harvest?* Grand Rapids: Zondervan, 1975.

Feucht, Oscar E. *Everyone a Minister.* St. Louis: Concordia, 1974.

France, R.T. *I Came to Set the Earth on Fire.* Downers Grove: Inter Varsity Press, 1975.

Gerber, Virgil. *God's Way to Keep a Church Going and Growing.* Glendale: Regal, 1973.

Getz, Gene A. *Loving One Another.* Wheaton: Victor, 1979.

Getz, Gene A. *Sharpening the Focus of the Church.* Chicago: Moody Press, 1974.

Hadidian, Allen. *Successful Discipling.* Chicago: Moody Press, 1979.

Hartman, Doug, and Doug Sutherland. *A Guidebook to Discipleship.* Irvine: Harvest House, 1976.

Hendricks, Howard G. *Say it With Love.* Wheaton: Victor, 1972.

Henrichsen, Walter A. *Disciples Are Made Not Born.* Wheaton: Victor, 1974.

Jennings, Alvin. *3 R's of Urban Church Growth.* Fort Worth: Star Bible, 1981.

Kittel, Gerhard, ed. *Theological Dictionary of the New Testament.* Grand Rapids: Eerdmans, 1967.

Kuhne, Gary W. *The Dynamics of Discipleship Training.* Grand Rapids: Zondervan, 1978.

Kuhne, Gary W. *The Dynamics of Personal Follow-Up.* Grand Rapids: Zondervan, 1976.

Lewis, C.S. *Mere Christianity,* New York: MacMillan, 1943.

Lucas, Chuck. "Lifestyle Evangelism." *At the Crossroads,* 24:5:1, February 8, 1981.

MacDonald, William. *True Discipleship.* Kansas City: Walteric, 1975.

McGavran, Donald, and Win Arn. *How to Grow a Church.* Glendale: Regal, 1973.

McKenna, David L. *The Jesus Model*. Waco: Word, 1977.

McPhee, Arthur G. *Friendship Evangelism*. Grand Rapids: Zondervan, 1978.

Metzger, Will. *Tell the Truth*. Downers Grove: Inter Varsity Press, 1981.

Moore, Waylon B. *New Testament Follow-Up: For Pastors and Laymen*. Grand Rapids: Eerdmans, 1963.

Olbricht, Thomas H. *The Power to Be*. Austin: Sweet, 1979.

Petersen, William J. *The Discipling of Timothy*. Wheaton: Victor, 1980.

Peterson, Eugene H. *A Long Obedience in the Same Direction*. Downers Grove: Inter Varsity Press, 1980.

Phillips, J.B. *The New Testament in Modern English*. New York: MacMillan, 1958.

Phillips, Keith. *The Making of a Disciple*. Old Tappan: Fleming H. Revell, 1981.

Pippert, Rebecca Manley. *Out of the Salt Shaker and Into the World*. Downers Grove: Inter Varsity Press, 1979.

Pippert, Rebecca Manley. *Pizza Parlor Evangelism*. Downers Grove: Inter Varsity Press, 1976.

Shipp, Stanley. "What For?" Sermon at White River Christian Camp, Crosbyton, Texas. Tape available at Church of Christ Student Center, Lubbock, Texas.

Stott, John. *Focus on Christ*. Great Britain: Collins, 1979.

Stott, John R.W. *Basic Christianity*. Downers Grove: Inter Varsity Press, 1958.

Survey on Discipleship. Information collected by Milton Jones for a dissertation at California Graduate School of Theology, January, 1982.

Taylor, Richard Shelly. *The Disciplined Life*. Minneapolis: Dimension, 1962.

Vigeveno, H.S. *Jesus, the Revolutionary*. Glendale: Regal, 1966.

Warr, Gene. *You Can Make Disciples*. Waco: Word, 1978.

Wilson, Carl. *With Christ in the School of Disciple Building*. Grand Rapids: Zondervan, 1976.